PRAISE FOR:

An Agent Speaks: A Primer for Unpublished Writers

Joan West who is an author, publisher, agent gives in "An Agent Speaks a Primer for Unpublished Writers" practical advice to novice writers who need to know about this industry. West explains the process of getting an agent, finding the right agent, self-publishing a book, marketing, and lots of other things new writers do not know. "An Agent Speaks: A Primer for Unpublished Writers" is a wealth of information for new writers to help them avoid making costly mistakes.

Gary Roen
Reviewer
The Midwest Book Review

Other Books by Joan West

Novels:

Call of the Loon

Nonfiction:

An Agent Speaks:
A Primer for Unpublished Writers

Edited:

The First Annual Journal
of The Creative Writers Notebook

The Second Annual Journal
of The Creative Writers Notebook

CATS: A book of short stories about cats

HOW TO SELL YOUR BOOKS:

A PUBLISHER SPEAKS

Helping Writers Succeed

Joan West, Ph.D.

AimHiPress Publishing Company
Lady Lake, Florida

www.how2sellyourbooks.com

Joan West

Printed in the United States of America

Cover Designer David Stone
Publishing Consultant Joshua Newhouse

Published by
AimHiPress
Lady Lake, Florida 32159
www.aimhipress.com

ISBN-13:
978-1502902979

ISBN-10:
1502902974

Acknowledgements

I want to thank all the professionals who have contributed information to this book. They have helped enormously to clarify the terms and information I've set down in these chapters. They have also contributed to the validity of the contents. Thanks: Leanne Burroughs, Bobbi Christmas, Olive Church, Olivia Claire High, Martha Jeffers, Chrissy Johnson, Linda Masek, Jim McGann, Jamie Morris, Mark Newhouse, Claudette Parmenter, Mary Lois Sanders, Peter Shianna, Carole Stuart, Linda terBurg Allen Watson and Tom Wallace.

I also owe a great debt to my partner and friend, Lois Bennett. She is not only a professional through and through, but she demonstrates a practical side that helps to keep me from going overboard. Thanks, Lois.

Finally, thanks to my husband, Glen, the moderator of The Villages Creative Writing Group for the past fourteen years. He took over the reins in 1998 when its founder Allen Gold passed away, but refused to sit in Allen's chair. Although we don't always agree on the best word here, or where to put a comma, I have to admit that his editing skills have saved me from many a goof, not that I don't continue to make them here and there in spite of his advice. His frequent suggestions to back away and take a breath have often saved my sanity. Every writer knows what I mean.

Joan West

Table of Contents

CHAPTER ONE

I WANT TO HELP YOU SUCCEED

WHY I WROTE THIS BOOK?

This book is about helping writers succeed. It's about helping *you* succeed. As a first effort toward this goal, I wrote a book called: *An Agent Speaks: A Primer for Unpublished Writers.* That book was based on what I had learned as a literary agent in partnership with Lois Bennett.

WHY I BECAME A PUBLISHER?

Lois and I decided a better way to achieve our mission of helping writers become published authors would be to move from being agents to becoming publishers and Fireside Publications was born.

HOW WAS BEING A PUBLISHER DIFFERENT THAN BEING AN AGENT?

Wearing our new hats, we encountered a new set of problems, all requiring research and new solutions if we were to be successful in this challenging venture.

HOW WILL MY EXPERIENCES HELP YOU?

I don't pretend to know it all, but during my years as a publisher, I've learned a lot, and it's this information I want to share with you—information which includes what I know about traditional publishing, including small press publishing, and what I've learned about self-publishing, and about getting published in general. By the time you finish this book, that knowledge will be yours to help you accomplish your goal of becoming a published writer.

WHY IS IT IMPORTANT TO READ THIS BOOK NOW?

Self-publishing and e-books have become the twenty-first century's answer to book publishing. If you don't get in on it now, you may be left out of the marketplace. People haven't stopped reading; they have just changed how they do it.

In addition to producing a book full of new information to help you achieve your goals, as a bonus for those of you who want to pursue the services of an agent, I have included material from pertinent chapters in *An Agent Speaks*. Essentially, you will find that material in Chapter Nine (How to prepare a query package for fiction) and Chapter Ten (How to prepare a proposal for nonfiction.

Whatever routes you choose, I wish you every success in your writing career.

WHAT AREAS WILL WE DISCUSS?

I

I have tried to include the most important elements you need to be successful in publishing and marketing your book. You will find many suggestions, some of my personal rules, and a few anecdotes from my experiences as an agent and a publisher. I am also pleased to offer select "nuggets of wisdom" from other generous
* writers
* publishers
* writing coaches
* editors
* writing group leaders

and other contributors who are integral to the workings of the industry and the success of writers.

HOW YOU CAN USE THIS BOOK?
Most of the material in the book falls into three categories:
- writing
- publishing
- marketing

Structuring the book like this would have impeded the flow, but you can concentrate on each category by noting the chapters below:

WRITING: Chapters 2, 3, 9, 10, 11, 17, 18

PUBLISHING: Chapters 4, 5, 6, 7, 8, 12

MARKETING: Chapters 13, 14, 15, 16

WARNING: Don't Rush to Submit.

Unless you have a photographic memory, you won't remember everything in these guidelines for submitting a manuscript. To get the most from this resource, please check back with the appropriate chapters before you submit. It may make the difference between having your manuscript accepted or dumped in the round file.

WARNING: Don't rush to self-publish.

Being thoroughly familiar with the different types of publishing houses, and what you can expect from each, as well as what you need to do for each, can make the difference in the content as well as the appearance of your self-published book, so please don't rush. I've seen too many authors regret not taking their time before they publish. I don't want you to be one of them.

ONE MORE CAVEAT

As complete as I have tried to make this text, one book probably won't do it. This book will get you started and help you avoid some of the pitfalls that you will face on your road to publication, but you will benefit from having others on your bookshelf, which is why I have included a list of helpful books in the Appendix. That's also why I've included a list of Resources—editors, book doctors—people to whom you might want to turn along the way. A list of web sites that might prove useful to you is also included along with a list of associations open to writers.

YOUR RESPONSIBILITY: DO YOUR HOMEWORK

Because I haven't read *all* of the books available, nor had personal experience with *all* the people and websites listed, and do not belong to *all* the associations, I cannot recommend them from personal experience, but have chosen to cite them confident that among them you will find books, individuals, web sites and associations which will aid you in your march to your goal. Remember, there is no substitute for diligent research before you take action.

WHY BOTHER WITH ALL THIS HARD WORK?

Writing a book is a major accomplishment. Publishing and marketing a book is hard work. So why do so many people do it?

Author Olive Church, says,"...I can't think of anything more satisfying than finishing a book and finally seeing it and holding it in your hands!"

If this book occasionally morphs into a cheering rally, I plead guilty. It's my belief that a writer needs all the encouragement available. My wish for you is that one day you will experience, as Olive has done, the once in a lifetime thrill of holding a book in your hands with your name imprinted boldly on the cover.

CHAPTER TWO

WHY DO YOU WRITE?

If a dozen writers were gathered together, you would find a dozen or more reasons for why they write. Many will agree with one of the greatest writers of modern times, Ernest Hemingway, when in 1940 he wrote in a letter to publisher Charles Scribner, *"I have to write to be happy whether I get paid for it or not."*

Hemingway's professed reason for writing is a lofty one and shared by many, if not most writers, but even those who agree, will often add another more prosaic reason or two.

THE WRITING BUG

Inveterate readers read—advertisements, lists, glossaries— whatever is available if a book is not. Inveterate writers write—wherever, whenever, whatever.

Writers wake up in the middle of the night with an idea, a phrase, just the right word they had been looking for the day before. Whatever it is, if you can't wait until morning to get it down on paper or typed into your computer, you know you're a writer. Even in the dead of winter, when the heat has been turned down, you throw off the covers and pad in your slippers to wherever you keep your computer or your paper and pen.

You can't rest until you see it written. You have the 'writing bug'.

Let's take a look at some of the other reasons writers give for writing.

I WANT TO BE RICH AND FAMOUS

How realistic is this as a reason to write?

We know about the successes of the Stephen Kings, the Nora Roberts and the Nicholas Sparks, but what about most writers?

The truth is the books of far more writers end up in the bargain books catalogues at a fraction of the cover price the year after publication. The writers of these 'mid-list' books (books which fall between best sellers and the classics), may get a contract for a second book or even a third, especially if they write to a particular niche, but unless they have a private income, they keep their day jobs.

Many writers would give the kitchen sink to have one, two or three books published with any monetary return. Unfortunately, that may not happen.

The point is: Be realistic about your chances of becoming one of the wealthy and famous authors. It may happen, but this should not be your sole motivation for writing.

FAME?

As with becoming 'rich', not every published writer's name becomes a household word.

J. K. Rowling, John Grisham and Danielle Steele are well-known names, but take another look through that bargain books catalogue. How many writers' names do you see listed there—all published authors, but whose names or titles you've never heard of?

It certainly is not my intention to discourage you before you even begin. On the other hand, one of my tasks in this book is to provide you with the realities of publishing, as well as the means to become published. I would not be honest if I promised your writing guarantees you fame and fortune.

If the act of writing satisfies, gives you a sense of accomplishment, then go for it. You just may be the author of the next best seller and achieve your dream of being rich and famous. But first write because you love it.

I WANT TO PROMOTE SOMETHING CLOSE TO MY HEART

Many writers write to express a passion, to fight for a cause. They hope to win the support of others in their battle.

The cause could be broadly defined, such as, cancer, abuse or hunger. Some writers specialize in specific areas within these 'general' causes: e.g. lung cancer, child abuse or hunger in the Appalachians.

In all of these cases, the motivation for writing is to express passion and spread knowledge to gain support and express one's concerns.

FIGHTER FOR A CAUSE

Mary J. Stevens, a former nun belonging to the Order of the Sisters of St. Joseph, wrote *Blessed: My Battle with Brain Disease*, after suffering for years with an undiagnosed illness. Her book is a good example of writing to advance a cause.

When her health forced her to leave the convent, Mary returned home, continuing to teach, but now doing so as a lay teacher in her local parochial school. She eventually married and, although told she could never have children, went on to have three normal healthy babies, now healthy, successful adults.

Following years of tests and excruciating pain, an off-hand remark she made to her doctor—that she had an identical twin—led to a diagnosis of acromegaly. If you have never heard the term, you are not unusual. Acromegaly is defined as: a hormonal disorder usually resulting from a benign pituitary tumor where the pituitary gland produces an excess of a growth hormone (GH).

It is because you and most of the rest of the population have never heard of the disease that Mary wrote the book. She discovered that this condition is frequently misdiagnosed. Repeatedly, she was told her problems were "all in her head", it was the flu and, by a physician who offered to remedy the situation, "You need sex!"

Mary took her personal experience and decided to share it with others to help them. She feels passionately about the many people she believes suffer, as she did, from a lack of an accurate diagnosis.

Did she become rich and famous through the publication of her book? She hadn't the last time I spoke with her. Did she derive satisfaction that acromegaly groups ordered copies of the book and that individuals read it? Yes. And she doesn't regret the time she spent researching and writing the book because of the sense of accomplishment she receives knowing it is helping others.

THE EXPERT ADVANTAGE

A good example of the writer who is an expert in her cause was Rachel Carson. Her credentials were a major advantage in getting her books published and becoming well known.

17

Rachel Carson wrote *The Silent Spring* and subsequent books out of her passion for the ecology, and what she saw happening to it. Like Mary Stevens, she wrote out of passion, but with one very big difference: Mary wrote from her own suffering and perspective, Rachel was a professional—an expert in her field.

After Rachel graduated from Chatham University (formerly The Women's College of Pennsylvania), she did graduate work at Johns Hopkins University where she earned her reputation as a marine biologist and environmentalist.

Writing as an 'expert' in a field you are passionate about gives you certain advantages over someone who does not have those credentials. Mary's platform (see Chapter Nine for description of platform for fiction authors or Chapter Ten for non-fiction authors) was limited to personal experience, not always enough for a nonfiction platform where expertise and professional experience are highly valued by publishers, but, as in Mary's case, her personal experience, her passionate research, and her willingness to share and help others made her book a valuable contribution and something she had to do. Even if it never made her rich or famous, the need to tell her story, and her sense of accomplishment when she finally saw it in print, made her efforts worthwhile.

PUBLISH OR PERISH

Yet a slightly different example of why a writer writes is the academic who must publish to keep his job, and in turn, build the reputation of his institution. This is the 'publish or perish' academic writer, but also relates to the 'status' writer, the writer who writes because it is required, or expected, by his/her profession, or because it is a symbol of status, and affirmation of their being an expert.

Scan the faculty list of any university and you will see a list of publications beside the name of each faculty member. The more prestigious the institution, the more important the publications must be, and the greater the pressure to publish, especially if it brings in money for grants and research.

We can argue the merits of publish and perish on teaching universities forever. I would like to believe that much, probably most, of the academic writing that faculty members produce is from a sincere interest in their subject, and that they have a genuine desire to write about their field, nevertheless, if you must write to keep your job, you write. Hopefully, you do so also because you care about your subject and have much to add. If you are successful, you may achieve status as an expert in your field.

I'M AN EXPERT WHO WANTS TO PASS ON KNOWLEDGE

In this category, so many names pop quickly into my mind: Andrew Weil, M.D. and Deepak Chopra, M.D. for example. Both men have medical degrees but use their expertise in different areas of mind and body health. Clearly Doctors Weil and Chopra are dedicated to passing their knowledge on to the reading public. Imagine what a loss it would be if they, and other experts, did not write what they have learned in their years of research and experimentation?

Experts in writing, who possess a passion for their profession and who write about it for the benefit of other writers, abound.[1]

One of the best and most useful references for writers, is *Self-Editing for Fiction Writers: How to edit yourself into print* by Renni Browne and Dave King. Since having your work edited is a must, this book will put you ahead of the game. But how do we know it is written by 'experts'?

On the cover of the paperback edition, we're told Ms. Browne worked as a senior editor for William Morrow, Mr. King, served as a contributing editor at *Writer's Digest Magazine* and an independent editor in New England. Their educational and professional credentials help establish them as experts in their field. Writers are lucky they have cared enough to share their knowledge.

Doctors Weil and Chopra and editors Browne and King are well known and experienced in their fields, but a yet unpublished expert can share his/her specialist information as well. And for many, this is the most promising route to publication. But being an expert is not necessarily a guarantee of fame and fortune.

Attorney John R. Howard, a retired Distinguished Service Professor from the State University of New York (SUNY), is also the recipient of a national Endowment for the Humanities focus Grant for a program on African American Art and Culture. As such, Professor Howard did extensive research and became an expert on the professional lives of two eminent African American film producers: Oscar Micheaux and Spike Lee. He shares his extensive knowledge of his subjects with readers in his book, *Faces in the Mirror: Oscar Micheaux & Spike Lee*. But is he famous?

The similarity between Weil, Chopra and Howard is that they have all spent years researching and becoming 'experts' in their fields. Weil and Chopra are well-known, while Howard is as yet not widely known. "As yet" is the operative phrase.

1 in my opinion, all writers should have a library of books on writing and add to it constantly. If you don't know what's available, go to your local bookstore and look on the shelves or go to www.*Writers Digest.com* for an unending variety of resources for writers.

Unlike Howard, Doctors Weil and Chopra have a wide 'platform', people know their name and associate it with their area of expertise. Their publishers know that any book they publish is going to be purchased the minute it hits the bookstores—print or electronic.

You, and Professor Howard, don't have that assurance 'as yet', but if your expertise is well grounded, and you learn the secrets of effective marketing, (covered in this book and in AimHiPress's, How To Sell Your Books Checklist and Marketing Workbook), you may have the next great expert book. At any rate, writing about what you are an expert in gives you a significant advantage. It is definitely something to consider before you decide what you want to write about.

WHY I WRITE? FILL IN THE BLANK

We've discussed some of the most cited reasons why writers write: to be happy, rich and famous, to promote something close to your heart, to publish or perish or to share your knowledge, but a group of other motivations are also frequently mentioned, and may be just as important in answering why you write.

One of my writer friends told me writing gives her a sense of identity. She is not just the mother of Catherine or the sister of John or the ex-wife of Neils. She isn't "just a housewife." She says she loves to write, but more important, it makes her feel productive. "When someone asks me what I do, I can say, 'I'm a writer' and I stand up a little straighter."

"I'm never bored," says another writer. "When I'm writing, I'm in another world—a new world—a world of my imagination—I can go wherever I want to, do whatever I want to, be whatever I want to be."

Joan West

For myself, I like the independence that writing gives me. I can set my own hours and I am my own task master—a harder one than any boss I ever had when working a nine-to-five job; but that's okay because while my failures are my own, so are my accomplishments. It's both empowering and humbling for a writer to acknowledge that her successes truly are her own and when she blows it, the responsibility is hers alone.

I WANT TO BE SUCCCESSFUL

Whatever you write, every author wants to feel successful, but how do you define success?

You may be able to fill in the blank of why you choose to write, with an assortment of reasons, the ones cited above, or many more, but whatever your motivation, you've decided to write and want success. So how do we measure it? How are you going to know that you have achieved that goal?
 When you've written a book?
 When you've published a book?
 When you can support yourself and your family on what you earn as a writer?
Maybe you said you want to be rich. How do you measure "rich"?
 When you earn $100,000 per year?
 When you are a millionaire?
 When you earn enough to afford an apartment on Fifth Avenue in New York and can take time off to travel and take taxis whenever you want to? When you can light cigars with twenty dollar bills?

I'm rooting for you and want to see you succeed, but believe you'll have a much better chance of success if you define it in terms you can measure.

So humor me. Go back and state your reason for writing, followed by how you'll know when you get there. Be specific.

Set goals that are realistic. Set short term goals, and if you are brave, set long term goals that you feel define success. (See How To Market Your Books Checklist for goal-setting worksheet.)

WHERE DO WE GO FROM HERE?

Okay, you now know why you write. You have set your short term and career goals, and you know how you'll be able to tell when you reach your goals. So let's get on with it. Turn the page and let's talk about what you are going to write.

CHAPTER THREE

WHAT DO YOU WRITE?

In the last chapters, you determined that you are a *writer* and you know *why* you write; equally important is *what* you write.

If you are already writing, already begun a book or have a completed one, you already know what you write. Or do you?

There are so many different categories and genres that you may be having difficulty knowing exactly where your book fits.

You may also be wondering if you are writing in the best genre for you, or if you can achieve success by writing in more than one genre.

FICTION vs NON-FICTION

All writing can be divided into these two categories:
fiction and non-fiction.

Fiction are creations largely from the imagination, but may be based on real events, people, or issues, while non-fiction must adhere to the facts, reality, and often requires expertise or research for its success.

Even historic fiction is very dependent on the realities that underlie the story, and the author can be taken to task when he departs a tad too much from 'what really happened'.

In this chapter, I'm going to list some of the genres and categories in which works of fiction or nonfiction are written. There are some issues about how absolute these genre are and I'm not sure anyone in the business could write about this area of publishing with absolute definitions that will not be , but at least you should have some sense of what fits where, and what opportunities different genre offer.

FICTION

For many first time authors, genre fiction may seem the easiest and most popular of all types of fiction to write. But even here competition is great and knowledge is critical if you wish to succeed.

Essentially, genre fiction is formulaic: it usually has a beginning, middle and ending. It is the structure most of us are familiar with in mysteries, fairy tales and narratives of all kinds.

It begins with a **'Convention'**—
A crime has been committed, a disaster is unfolding, a young woman is unattached with no romance on the immediate horizon. The conflict or problem is stated.

It continues with a **'Middle'**-
Clues begin to appear, a hero moves into the scene, a young man emerges—often our young woman hates him on sight.

And it concludes with an **'Ending'**-
The crime is solved, the main characters in the disaster are rescued and the young woman and the young man fall in love and marry. And hopefully live happily ever after...or maybe not?

Genre fiction is popular, and, properly written, published and marketed, may move off the shelf quickly. The names of many genre novel authors have become household words, with huge fan clubs, the members of which hold their breaths awaiting the next offering of their favorite author. It could be you if you learn your craft and practice it.

Genre novels are fairly specific in their word count: i.e. most ranging in word count from 65,000 to 80,000 words, rarely surpassing 100,000 words.

*A bit of important information for a first time writer: Watch your word count, not your page count. Page count can differ due to type size, margin width, how far down on the page your chapter heading falls, if you begin new chapters always on the right hand page or if you begin a new chapter on the page immediately following the conclusion of the previous chapter and other such variables.

GENRES OF FICTION CATEGORIES

Genre novels fall into a number of categories: romance, mystery, adventure, horror, science fiction, new age, western, and the new chick lit.

And there may be more as the need arises.

And it doesn't stop there. Each of the above genres have sub-genres:

Romance Genre includes highly popular subgenres: contemporary, historic romance, paranormal romance, and even romantic suspense. Any one of these could come under the heading of what is popularly called "bodice ripping romance".

Not only does each genre have its sub-genres, but each sub-genre has its own set of parameters, especially where word count is concerned. This can become confusing so my advice: If you plan to submit to Harlequin or any of the other romance houses, be sure to find out, *before* you write your book, exactly what their guidelines are for your specific genre. Visit their site on-line and look for 'submissions guidelines'. It could make the difference between selling your book or a quick rejection.

MAINSTREAM COMMERCIAL NOVELS

Probably the largest and most popular category after the genre novels is the mainstream /commercial division.

Unless your novel fits into one of the specific genres, it probably is mainstream, almost all of which are aimed for the commercial market.

These books are written for the general reading public and are geared to be commercial. They may focus on almost any topic: feminist, religious, dramas of all kinds. Almost all are written to be commercial, which means they are intended to sell well and hopefully provide a profit for the publishers and excellent royalties for their authors. Not that all books aren't hopeful money-makers, but as you will see later, sometimes profit is secondary as a goal.

It should be understood that publishing is a business and these books are specifically the ones the publisher feels are worthy of investment. In many cases, these are 'the name, authors' whose name alone almost guarantee sales. These are the books for which publishers reserve the better part of their advertising budgets. They are the books whose authors are sent on cross-country tours at the publishers' expense and whose authors make the rounds of the major television talk shows.

While every author dreams of this kind of commercial success, it may not come with the first book, or ever. But that should not stop you from achieving your goals as a writer. You may be the one who finds that combination of story, character, theme that makes your book the next best-seller.

LITERARY NOVELS

Literary novels tend to be more complicated, and to carry a message. Epic themes often appear as well as richly detailed characters. These novels are almost always longer than their cousins in the mainstream; however, while not 'targeted' for the commercial category, they may still become best sellers because their quality becomes recognized or they hit a universal theme. Some become the award-winners, another way of achieving success.

For example, take a look at some of John Updike's work, never intended to become 'best sellers', *Couples*, and his two Pulitzer Prize winners, *Rabbit is Rich* and *Rabbit at Rest reached those heights because of the quality of his writing and the universality of his themes*, rather than their being targeted for commercial success as in genre fiction.

Also in this category are such women writers: as Toni Morrison and Joan Didion. Try Morrison's *Beloved*, also a Pulitzer Prize winner, and Didion's *Run, River, and you will see books not considered mainly commercial or mainstream that became best-sellers again because of their quality, their passion at dealing with their subject.*

The moral is that you should write, not to be commercial as your primary goal, but to create a quality book about something you care about.

MY NOVEL IS NONE OF THE ABOVE

In addition to those novels which fall neatly into these main designations, some don't quite fit, but may have a specialized reading audience of their own.

Some examples: stories with an animal as the main character, gay and lesbian novels, historical novels, juvenile and young adult novels and fictionalized biographies and autobiographies.

These last two categories demonstrate how genre are constantly evolving, having sprung from biographies and autobiographies, primarily because their authors have, in the case of biographies, developed scenes and dialog they couldn't possibly have known from research.

If authors of these types of books are good at their craft, they adhere as much as possible to 'fact', but elect to use 'story form' and 'reasonable literary license', for easier, more enjoyable reading. Often this can help an author make a difficult, painful subject understandable to a younger audience than a straight biography/autobiography.

For example, when Ruth Treeson, wrote her autobiography, *The Long Walk*, as a young adult novel, she felt that she could not precisely portray the dialog needed to give the story interest so she felt compelled to enhance the dialog, moving the category from straight biography to 'fictionalized biography', or if the departure is more fictional, 'historical fiction'.

Ruth's story begins with her liberation at age fifteen from a prison camp during the holocaust in Nazi Germany and follows her frightening, but eventually triumphant journey from the camp to what had been her home in Poland and on to the United States. The events are true, but written as a novel to be suitable for her intended audience, and to fill in the gaps that can no longer be filled in by the actual participants in the historical event.

Joan West

MIXED GENRES?

This is a misnomer. There is no such thing as a 'mixed' genre according to publishing references. Unfortunately, It actually reveals an author who lacks experience and hasn't done their research before submitting their work.

I have received submissions from writers who proudly tell me how wonderful their work is because they haven't written in just one genre; their wonderful book is different from any other. It's a combination of romance, history, fantasy and horror.

I always wonder why these writers haven't asked themselves why it is that no other writers have thought to write a 'mixed genre' such as this before? Unfortunately, it is obvious this writer has obviously never read a book on the subject or he would know better than to submit with a category that makes the publisher/agent unable to sell or publish such a book.

The sad truth is when something like this comes across my desk, it immediately goes into its self-addressed-stamped-envelope (SASE) and into the return mail. I feel badly about these writers and would like to respond, and enlighten them about genre and mixed genre, and on a few occasions I've managed to find the time to do so, but agents and editors can't squeeze the time out of their heavy schedules to do this on a regular basis.

Please understand, it is not an agent or editor's job to educate a writer in the basics.

So you must know your genre. It could very well fall into one of the sub-genres, such as historical romance or true crime, but it must fit into one of the recognized categories for an agent or publisher to accept it, or even look at it. There are several good books that list and define these classifications. I strongly suggest you determine which genre applies to your work before you submit to an agent or publisher.

NONFICTION

As I stated earlier, nonfiction works depend on fact, truth and reality. It is the author's responsibility to adhere to these standards by careful research and accurate reporting.

The success of a nonfiction book often depends on the credentials and reputation of the author, so often these books are written by 'experts' or those who have the passion to do the research that is essential for the subject. It is a highly popular market, with a high demand for writers willing to devote themselves to this field.

Books of nonfiction divide themselves into as many categories as there are topics to write about.

Some nonfiction categories:
autobiographies/memoirs,
biographies,
histories,
philosophy,
psychology,
sociology,
animals,
crime,
politics

and the list goes on...

A word of warning:
Do not confuse fictionalized biography with biography and fictionalized autobiography/memoir with autobiography. I'm sure you have read about a couple of writers in the recent past who have crossed over the line between the two. They violated the basic tenets of nonfiction and were accused of a lack of integrity.

If you are going to write about your, or someone else's life, autobiography or biography, you must write truthfully. Don't exaggerate to create more interest and don't fill in the gaps with your creative inventions. Nonfiction is just that, and once you depart from the truth, you are writing fiction.

So why do some authors knowingly submit fiction as nonfiction, knowing the risk of being caught?

It is easier to get published with nonfiction if you find the right subject and can convince a publisher you have the facts. Many writers shy away from the demands of research, the years of preparation, for successful nonfiction so there may be less competition and an easier path, very tempting to someone who wants success, but isn't willing to adhere to the requisites of nonfiction.

If you want to depart from the truth in biography/autobiography, then write a piece of pure fiction based on your life or the life of someone who intrigues you, changing names and whatever else is necessary to disguise the characters, and be certain you make it clear to yourself and others this work is fiction.

WHERE DO WE GO NEXT?

At this point, you know why you write and what you write. Now, what are you going to do with that manuscript?

Obviously, you want to have it published. That's what it's all about, isn't it? So the next step is to determine how you're going to do that....

Should you publish traditionally? What type of publishers are available? What can you expect from a major publishing house? What are the advantages of a small press?

Chapter Four will explore the differences among publishers, and Chapter Five will give you an idea of what you can expect from the traditional publishing houses. Let's get to it!

CHAPTER FOUR
TRADITIONAL PUBLISHING HOUSES:
The Majors, the Mid-Sized and the Minors

WHAT IS TRADITIONAL PUBLISHING?

First, let's be clear on what being published traditionally means. It's very simple. Traditional publication means your manuscript has been given to an editor at a publishing house which has agreed to publish it at _no cost_ to you.

Now, let's say you have decided you want to submit your work to a traditional publishing house. Okay, but what type of house do you propose to approach? Essentially you will find the industry divided into three types of houses, depending roughly on size: the majors (the largest), the mid-sized houses and the small presses. Each has advantages and disadvantages you should know about.

THE MAJORS

The major publishing houses are usually large corporations, even divisions of conglomerates: Hachette Book Group, Harlequin, HarperCollins, MacMillan, Penguin Group, Random House, and Simon & Schuster. These are the blockbusters of the publishing industry.

Each of these majors is divided into several independent **imprints** which you should know about since they may specialize in specific types of books.

IMPRINTS

For example, Little, Brown and Company is an imprint of Hachette. Silhouette and Steeple Hill are just two of the imprints at Harlequin, each with several of their own specific imprints. HarperCollins is divided into eight principal imprints, each offering its own set, for example, listed under Harper Morrow we find Avon and Ecco among over a dozen others. Henry Holt and St. Martin's Press are two of McMillan's imprints. Riverhead is only one of those belonging to the Penguin Group. Crown Trade Group and Knopf Doubleday Publishing Group fall under the aegis of Random House. Simon & Schuster splits itself up into Simon & Schuster Adult Publishing, Simon & Schuster Children's Publishing and Simon & Schuster International.

It is not easy to get considered by one of these mega-publishing houses. If you have dreams of being published by one of these giants, you will have to obtain the services of an agent since the major publishing houses will not accept submissions or queries directly from an author. Unfortunately, obtaining the services of an agent is almost as difficult as being published by any one of the houses listed above. (See Chapter Six)

MID-SIZED PUBLISHING HOUSES

Mid-sized publishing houses, as you might expect, are smaller than the majors, but are often more accessible to author submissions than their larger brothers.

Examples of Mid-sized Publishing Houses

McBooks Press might be considered a mid-sized publisher. Located in Ithaca, New York (www.mcbooks.com), they publish both fiction and nonfiction and will look at submissions directly from the author, as well as from agents.

A few years ago, when Lois Bennett, and I were partners in Bennett & West Literary Agency, Lois placed a book with them. She found them to be efficient and easy to work with. Be sure to check out their web site for guidelines before submitting to them. You should always check out the specific publisher/agent websites for their latest guidelines since they change frequently.

Often these publishers demonstrate their accessibility by offering help to authors who wish to submit.

Carole Stuart, the publisher of Barricade Books, Inc. (www.barricadebooks.com), reads submissions sent to her company directly from authors. Her key advice to writers: "Make your submission 'reader friendly." Like other publishers, she tells exactly what she expects in a submission:

> *Write a brief cover letter telling the title and subject matter of the book. Enclose a stamped return addressed envelope for a reply. I no longer respond if I don't get that. We get too many submissions and we tend to reply when it's easy for us."*

> *"Enclose an outline and a few chapters—very few—from your book. If we want to see more, we'll ask for it."*

> *Last—and perhaps first—make sure you know the kind of books the publisher publishes."*

Stuart says emphatically.

> *We don't do any fiction, poetry or novellas, but still get submissions. That shows me the writer didn't do her/his job."*

Having your manuscript accepted by one of these houses is a real coup, but even that is not necessarily a done deal. Let me tell you the story of a writer I know.

The 'Done Deal' Undone

With his first novel accepted by one of the major publishing houses, our Writer X began to work with the editor assigned to him. All went well. Oh, they had their discussions about one point or another throughout the manuscript, but were able to come to agreement until the editor suggested he needed to rework the ending.

They went back and forth and back and forth discussing what the editor perceived was a problem and the author's rationale for sticking with the ending as he wrote it.

Finally, the contract was cancelled by mutual agreement.

Writer X was unalterably opposed to changing what he considered to be an appropriate conclusion to his story. His thinking went something like this: If this major publishing house had accepted his novel, surely another would, and a new editor would see the value of his original ending. Wrong!

The only house which now showed any interest in publishing the book was a small press, whose offer he accepted.

What would you do in this situation? When you sell a book to a publisher, you may have to face this kind of decision and only you know how you will react.

HOW DO I FIND MID-SIZED PUBLISHERS

For a list of mid-sized publishers, who are more apt to accept submissions directly from the authors, check out the Book Publishers' pages in the most recent copy of *Writer's Market*. By the way, if you don't already purchase the yearly updated copy of this publication, go right out and get it. (for more about this and other publications all writers should have on their bookshelves see Chapter Seventeen)

THE SMALL PRESSES

While we may dream of being published by the larger publishers, for most of us, the small presses present greater accessibility. Most will accept unsolicited manuscripts, submissions from un-agented authors and offer an easier path to being published.

The annual issue of *Writer's Market*, contains an entire section listing small presses (many pages of them!) and, incidentally, you will also find a section listing Canadian and international book publishers that may also be accepting submissions.

EXAMPLE OF A SMALL PRESS

A good example of a small press house would be Highland Press Publishing located in High Springs, Florida. I've picked this press because my partner and I placed several books with them when we were literary agents. We found Leanne Burroughs the CEO to be helpful and easy to contact, a major plus in submitting to a small press.

Even with small presses, it is important to know what kinds of books they publish. At the time we worked with her, Highland Press only handled children's and romance material. Sometimes presses may change their needs. According to the listing in *Writer's Market*—confirmed by a look at Highland's attractive web site—they now have expanded and publish just about every area of fiction with the exception of erotica. (www.TheHighlandPress.com) Changing needs and requirements are one more reason why you need to check out a publisher carefully no matter the size of the house.

WORKING WITH A SMALL PRESS

Do I include illustrations?

Small presses may have smaller staff and resources: e.g. artists. A question that comes up frequently is about the advisability of submitting illustrations with a picture book. This can be answered by the publisher guidelines posted on their website.

For example, Highland Press wants illustrations to accompany children's books. This may be standard for a small press, but be aware that if you submit a children's story to the larger publishers, they usually have their own professional artists on staff and do not want your illustrations. So check this out carefully before you hire an illustrator and then find the publisher wants to use their own artists. This can be a costly mistake.

PUBLICITY

If you publish with a small press, chances are you will be entirely responsible for publicizing your book. You will have to set up your own radio and television and print interviews, as well as speaking engagements or any other type of advertising you may want to do—business cards, bookmarks, mailing pieces, etc. Although these services vary among individual small presses and authors are now expected to shoulder more of the weight for promotion with mid-size and larger presses as well.

QUALITY & SELECTIVITY

Don't think that because a publishing house is small it is easier to have your work accepted by them. Simply because they are small limits the number of books published yearly and because of this limited number of books, they are as careful in their choices as the big guys are.

Joan West

ADVANTAGES OF THE SMALL PRESS

Mary Lois Sanders is the publisher of Court Jester Press as well as a very useful newsletter, The Creative Writers' Notebook, and a short story contest and anthology series, (www.court jesterpublications.com). She is kind enough to share some advantages of working with a small press such as her own:

"Often an independent will specialize in a particular genre(s): romance; war and adventure; mystery, crime, thriller and intrigue; inspirational and spiritual, nonfiction, etc." For the author who specializes in a specific genre, it is a huge advantage to know which small press shares that passion.

Sanders also suggests that an advantage of working with an independent *"...is the one-on-one interest they take in marketing your books (with good cooperative distribution apparatuses, in con-junction with other independents)."* In other words, small publishers often network and cooperate with others to develop distribution and marketing opportunities so they can 'keep up with the big dogs'.

Finally, speaking from her experience as an editor and publisher, she continues, *"Perhaps the best working relationships between writers and editors are at these small houses, which take pride in finding new authors and publishing the best books possible."*

It is your job to research carefully before and after you submit your work. There are many good publishers in all these groups, but there are also those you may be better off avoiding.

Let's assume you have chosen to pursue the traditional route to publication. What can you expect from them? Chapter Five will give you a pretty good idea.

40

CHAPTER FIVE

<u>WHAT TO EXPECT FROM A TRADITIONAL PUBLISHER</u>

You have submitted your manuscript to a traditional publisher. You may have sent it directly to the editor or to an agent who performed that delightful task for you. Let's imagine that an editor has agreed to publish your book and you have received a contract. You're raring to go!

So What Can You Expect?

Working in various degrees of a partnership with you, the editor will edit your work (see Chapter Seven) and when both of you are satisfied, it goes to printing.

Let's look more closely at those procedures one step at a time:

THE CONTRACT

Your contract with the publishing house is the most important document that will pass between you and it other than your manuscript. It is important you understand it fully.

A contract is a written agreement. Be aware that if an item isn't in the contract, it *won't* be done. If it is in the contract, it <u>must</u> be done. A verbal promise, a hand shake, are not contracts.

What are some of the items that will appear in the standard contract?

RIGHTS GRANTED TO THE PUBLISHER

A contract gives rights to the publisher and states the publisher's obligations to the author.

If you want to withhold any particular right—the foreign rights, for example—it must be stated in the contract. Of course, realistically, a first time writer has little leverage to withhold any rights or to deviate from much of anything in the contract.

In a contract, it is important to note, "What you see is what you get," so be sure to understand fully all terms of the contract. Don't be afraid to ask questions.

STANDARD CONTRACT TERMS

Almost all contracts include the following:

OWNERSHIP STATEMENT:
A statement that the manuscript is wholly owned by you. A publisher wants to know the work is original and solely yours to sell...

DELIVERY DATE OF YOUR MANUSCRIPT:
The publisher wants to be assured you will deliver on your promises so you want to be sure that you can deliver a completed manuscript on time. This will include any rewrites.

REJECTION AND TERMINATION:
The publisher wants to assure his rights to reject work if the author fails to meet his deadline or if the work doesn't meet the publisher's standards.

APPROVAL OF COVER, ART & TITLE:
While a publisher may welcome, some consultation on the cover and the title of the book, they may protect their

investment by asserting control of these important promotional elements. Don't sign with a publisher until you are sure you are willing to cede these rights.

COMPENSATION: THE ADVANCE

The amount of the advance, if any, when it will be paid, and the percentage of royalties are of obvious interest to the author and should be clearly stated in your contract.

THE ADVANCE

An advance is a lump sum paid as an 'advance against royalties'. Sounds confusing? Let's look at an example.

Let's say you are offered a five thousand dollar advance for your book. Celebrate!

Not so fast!

You may receive this amount in one or two payments—half when you sign the contract, the remaining half on publication. Celebrate now?

Not so fast!

After publication, your royalties should begin, the amount based on your sales. The company will send periodic statements showing your sales and royalties, so now you can celebrate?

Not so fast! Where is my check?

You took an advance so you will not receive any real payment until the sales have made back the amount you were given as your **advance**. Then you can celebrate.

IS AN ADVANCE REFUNDABLE?

What happens if the book doesn't sell and it never makes back my advance?" Do I have to return the money?

Well, you won't receive any more checks. That's a given. However, I've never heard of a publishing house requiring an author to return the advance <u>if the author has satisfied the requirements of the contract</u>. I don't say it's never happened, just that I've never heard of it.

The five-thousand dollars mentioned above is fairly standard for a first book; however this amount can deviate from a couple thousand dollars to zilch. It will depend a great deal on the size of the publishing house and the author's track record.

WHAT IF I CAN'T GET AN ADVANCE?

Many small press publishers cannot afford to pay advances. You will notice that in the sample contract in the Appendix, no advance is mentioned. Remember, if an item isn't specifically stated in the contract, it doesn't exist.

Many authors, especially new ones, have to make a choice: accept a contract without an advance or keep trying until you find a publisher who may offer one to you. Frankly, in today's tight market, advances are hard to come by.

Royalties

Royalties are a percentage of the retail price paid to you, the author, by the publisher every time a book is sold.

For a first time writer, the royalty per book is usually seven and one half percent. E-books tend to have larger royalties: as high as forty percent depending on the publisher. Royalties are normally paid every six months, but timing may vary as stipulated in your contract.

OTHER CONTRACT ITEMS

The above items are essentially, the highlights of a standard contract. There are many other items you may want to consider. For an example of a standard literary contract between the publisher and the author, please see the Appendix. It is impossible in this book to go into detail about all aspects of contracts, so let's look at some helpers in this crucial aspect of writing.

CONTRACT HELP

AGENT

If you have an agent, he will look at the contract for you and it is to their advantage to get you the best terms possible since they are paid a percentage of your compensation. The good agent is experienced in standard publication contracts and should be able to guide you through it, but you should still be certain to understand every term and not go blindly into such an important endeavor.

LAWYERS

Should I get a lawyer?
I believe it's always a good idea to have an attorney look at the contract. If you can find one experienced in this particular field, so much the better, but check credentials carefully. Ask for references or google the attorney and see how others have fared. Remember, a good contract is based on your knowledge even if you are fortunate enough to 'land' an agent.

FREE LEGAL HELP

Among the organizations helping authors is the Authors' Guild **which offers free legal help to its members.**(www.authorsguild.org). A one year's membership for a writer earning $25,000 or less per year from his writing is currently $90. This organization offers several benefits, one of which is to review your contract and offer recommended contractual terms. In addition, among their many other benefits, they offer liability insurance, a website to list your books, tools to build a free web site which they will host for $6 per month. I must note that I do not belong to this organization at this time, but have had it recommended to me by a number of authors. The Authors' Guild is a non-profit professional organization that has been an avid advocate for author rights in a number of highly publicized cases against publisher practices. Its legal advice is well worth the price of membership.

YOUR EDITOR

A contract will require you to work positively with the editor assigned by your publisher. Specifics may vary, and the editor will not be named, but your lack of cooperation can be grounds for the termination of the contract. You should understand that in signing such a contract, you are ceding certain creative rights to the editor as representative of the publishing house.

Working with your editor can be touchy at times, but you must be able to complete your manuscript on time, which means you must be able to work with the assigned editor. In Chapter Seven I'll go into more detail about this important relationship.

INTERIOR DESIGN

Your contract will not describe the actual design of your book, but will give the final approval to the publisher so you must be willing to accept this loss of control.

Interior design is simply what the inside of the book looks like. Some books, primarily nonfiction books, require the use of charts, graphs, illustrations and/or photographs. The layout and attractiveness of these is the responsibility of the interior designer. They can make decisions about things we as authors never even imagine so ceding control to a 'pro' may have advantages, but could result in design features you may not love, but have to accept.

FOUR EXAMPLES OF INTERIOR DESIGN
AUTHORS NEVER THINK ABOUT

1. Mystery writer Dorothy L. Sayers' hard cover issue of *Whose Body*, sports a black rectangle at the top of each page that begins a new chapter. Within the rectangle, the designer placed the word CHAPTER (all caps and in white font) followed by a numeral. Further, the first letter of the first line of the chapters is oversized bold type and begins way over in the middle of the page rather than flush left at the usual indentation. What author would think of these design features? How do others handle them?

2. The designer of Ruth Rendell's *The Water's Lovely*, chose a completely different layout: Chapter One appears in caps and lower case—no numerals—and simply centered about a third down the page. A small diamond shaped symbol placed below the chapter heading provides focus.

3. A soft cover edition of Ernest Hemingway's *A Moveable Feast*, re-published in the 1990's, devotes a full page at the beginning of each chapter, centering the title of the chapter near the top of the page using italics, caps and lower case. Using a whole page? I never would have thought of that.

4. The first chapter, for example, is titled: *A Good Café on the Place St.-Michel*. These are the only words on the page. The chapters are not numbered, but the chapter title page is always a right hand page. The next page, a left-hand page, is left blank and the content of the chapter begins on the following right hand page. Very effective, but are authors trained to see these kinds of effects? Do we want to face these kinds of stylistic decisions?

THE BOTTOM LINE ON INTERIOR DESIGN

I've gone into considerable detail here, because interior design is something to which many authors don't give much thought. If you are being published traditionally, you may have to accept that you won't have much, if any input in the appearance of your book once you sign that contract.

But what if you hate it? Remember Writer X? By signing a contract you may be giving up all rights to protest the design. If you are lucky, the publisher might give you a hearing, but the final decision is one of the important rights you may have granted in your contract.

If this kind of control is important to you, you may want to consider self-publishing, but consider the examples above and your lack of training and experience in interior book design, and recognize how important the appearance of your book may be to its marketability before you decide for take all this on by yourself.

COPYRIGHT

Your contract will state who owns the copyright for your book. This is a right you must fully understand to protect you and your family's interests.

FORMAL VS INFORMAL COPYRIGHT

A formal copyright means you have taken the legal steps to register your ownership with the Federal Government's Copyright Office. This is essential if a book is to be published. An informal form of protection is automatically provided when your name and date appear on the work. On the following pages, we will discuss these various important ideas.

You will notice that all books contain a copyright page following the title page. The copyright page is a part of the interior design of the book that is extremely important. Several pieces of information will appear here, exactly how much depends on the author and the publisher, but the purpose is to clearly define what the book is and how it is protected.

The page will always contain:
- the name of the publishing house and its contact information,
- where the book was printed (US, other)
- the ISBN (a registration number)
- reproduction rights-
a line or a paragraph stating that neither the whole nor any part of the book may be reproduced followed by a list of ways in which it cannot be reproduced (in any form or by any electronic means...)
- and the copyright line.

Other information may be placed on this page, such as
*   the name of the cover designer, the interior designer, a photographer, etc.,

Most importantly, the copyright line and the ISBN *must* appear here.

An acceptable copyright line might read:

copyright 2012 by Bett A. Writer

or using the symbol: © 2012 Bett A. Writer

HERE IS THE POINT!

Be sure that it is your name that appears in the copyright line. You should own the copyright!!!

Most publishers will post that automatically, however, there are those who might attempt to put the name of the publishing house as the owners of the copyright which could create problems for the author. They are not the owners. You are. Read your contract carefully and do not cede this right.

SO WHO FILES A FORMAL COPYRIGHT?

If a publisher is going to file my copyright, should I?

A copyright filed with The Library of Congress is the ultimate protection. It keeps your material from being copied in whole or in part by anyone else without your permission. Generally speaking the responsibility of obtaining a copyright falls to the author.

Some debate surrounds the question of whether or not it is absolutely necessary for an author to obtain a formal copyright before submitting a work.

The argument for not bothering is that once the copyright symbol and notification appear on the Copyright Page of your book, it is automatically copyrighted according to international convention so why go through the expense and effort?

In a nutshell, the reverse argument asks, "Why take a chance?"

Since the Copyright Office has gone to the trouble of printing the various forms applicable to various means of copyrighting work and since the fee is reasonable, I recommend obtaining one. If someone does steal your writing, you would have an easier time defending it if you have formally registered it. In any event, take the time to check out their official web site: www.copyright.gov.

ANOTHER PROTECTIVE DEVICE: DISCLAIMERS

A disclaimer **may** help to protect a publisher/author from being sued. While such law suits are relatively rare, it is useful for you to understand how a disclaimer works. It is usually the author who creates the disclaimer prior to submitting his manuscript.

In one of the many excellent publications offered by his company ParaPubs, Dan Poynter offers a sample disclaimer from which you may design your own. (www.parapub.com).

In today's litigious society it is, sadly, a reasonable notice to post. I've adapted Dan's model and inserted a disclaimer at the back of this book. In my particular disclaimer, I want readers to understand the intent of this book is to provide information from my experiences, and not to give legal advice or to make "written in stone" statements, since so much in the publishing experience is in constant flux.

Please note: A disclaimer is not legal protection, but makes your intentions and limitations clear.

DO I NEED OTHER REGISTRATIONS FOR MY BOOK?

As we discussed, the initial copyright for your manuscript is your responsibility. You should always own your work, however many publishers, as part of their effort to protect their investment, will file the copyright and other registrations for you if they publish your book. All of this is stipulated in the contract and makes your job easier.

Simply put: Your contract makes registration of your book a responsibility of your publisher. So don't think because they are registering it, they are trying to steal it.

There are several places besides the Copyright Office where your book must be registered.

Bowkerlink

The publisher will list your book online at www.BowkerLink.com. This is the site of *Books in Print* and *Global Books in Print*, essential directories. Once the title of your book is listed here along with its ISBN and retail price, publisher and distributor, information about it can be accessed by anyone anywhere in the world. Self-publishers must register here on their own.

ISBN, EAN: MUST HAVES

Your publisher will arrange for an **ISBN number for your book.** An ISBN is required for every book published along with a Bookland EAN scanning symbol, more commonly known as a barcode, which includes the price of your book.

The **ISBN and barcode must be placed on the back cover of your book.** A self-publisher must obtain these on their own or their books will not be sold in bookstores and most on-line outlets. Take a look at the back several books and you will see where they appear.

THE COVER DESIGN

As we indicated, a publisher contract cedes your right to determine the cover design of your book. This may not be a bad thing.

If interior design is essential, the cover design is critical. Covers sell books.

Again, you must consider the differences in the amount of input you will have if you are publishing traditionally and giving up most, if not all, control, versus self-publishing (keep most control, depending on your method of self-publishing).

While designing a cover may appear simple, it requires many decisions and some authors welcome the experience and expertise of the traditional publisher as a trade-off for these many decisions. How much control are you willing to surrender is a critical factor in determining the course of publication you select.

An **author photo** and **bio** may or may not be placed on the cover or dust jacket of your book. In larger houses, the publisher will take care of writing the bio and of having a professional photograph taken. In today's reality, most small publishers and self-published authors must decide if this is advantageous to book sales and the author must take care of this themselves.

SUMMARY

All of the items above are important in the production of your book. Most are guaranteed in your contract. You should be able to expect all of the services cited above from a major or a mid-sized house, less perhaps from smaller ones. Each case may be different. Nothing is 'written it stone' so it's important to discuss exactly what services will be provided with a representative of your publisher and to be sure you read your contract carefully and ascertain that all aspects are included. Remember, if it isn't in your contract....

The important point is in all cases to understand how these different types of publishers work, the variations in services, and most importantly, to understand contracts are negotiable. So be sure to read and understand your contract before signing.

TRADITIONAL PUBLISHING:
ONE AUTHOR'S EXPERIENCE

Let's conclude this exploration of traditional publishing with an example of a real author's experience: Author Linda Lehmann Masek's experience with Avalon Books in New York (www.avalonboks.com).

Before Linda wrote her first adult novel, she had published a children's book, *Mag-ni-fi-cat* (now out of print), and had five children's articles published in magazines such as the well-known "Cobblestone" and "Children's Digest." She also was a collaborator on an *Encyclopedia of Cleveland History*.

Later, I published Linda's second novel *Soul Dance* set in Alaska. My partner, Lois, published her third, *The Serpent Sea* set in the Florida Keys. Both books are in the romantic suspense genre. As you can see she has a varied and promising history.

Here's what Linda said when I asked her about working with a major publisher like Avalon:

My first venture into adult publishing with a traditional publisher involved a romantic-suspense novel, The Poison Tree. I had submitted the first three chapters to Avalon Books in New York and received a form letter asking for the rest of the book. Upon submitting this, the editor for romantic-suspense novels, called me on the telephone to tell me Avalon wanted to publish my book! Needless to say, I was overjoyed!

"I learned more about Avalon Books; the publisher had been in business over one hundred years, having been founded by Thomas Bourgey. The books were all traditional, nonviolent hardbacks which relied on plot rather than excessive sexual encounters to create suspense. The publisher catered to a library market and published only in hardback. Different editors handled each category; Avalon produced several books per month including westerns, romantic-suspense, historical romance and mysteries.

"My contacts with Avalon were pleasant; after the initial call from my editor, who was interested in the pirate Blackbeard aspect of my story which was intrinsic to the mystery plot, I worked with her assistant, through a first draft with corrections. The book was published about a year later. Avalon Books paid an advance and I ordered at reduced cost, books to do my own

publicity in libraries and bookstores. Generally, I was pleased with the whole experience."

To add a postscript to Linda's story: Avalon Books has been sold to Amazon Publishers and she says, "I recently completed the paperwork to allow the new publisher of *The Poison Tree* to sell hardback books in print and on Kindle where it will soon be available (2012) worldwide. It seems I've become an 'Amazon Author' after almost ten years in 'print' at Avalon."

CONCLUSION

As with any dream, traditional publishing can be attained if you work hard, research carefully and do not give up. There are some negatives to traditional publishing such as the need to submit first to agents, the time from manuscript completion to acceptance, and ultimately to seeing a finished book compared to self-publishing, but Linda's story shows there may also be significant rewards. You need to weigh the positives against the negatives and decide how much control you want over your finished book before you sign that contract.

WHAT'S NEXT?

Let's get an agent!

CHAPTER SIX

ALL ABOUT LITERARY AGENTS

Some writers think of literary agents (henceforward, simply called "agents") as a necessary evil, but your agent can be your best friend—once you have one. Ah, thereby lies the problem: How do you find an agent willing to represent your work to the major publishers?

I covered this topic at some length in my book, *An Agent Speaks: A Primer for Unpublished Writers*. Most of this chapter was taken from that book with updates.

First, let's remove some of the mystery by looking at what you can expect from an agent.

WHAT AN AGENT CAN DO FOR YOU

First and foremost, an agent can submit your material to the large "glamour" publishing houses, most of which are located in New York with branches around the world principally in London or Ontario.

Even if these publishers agreed to accept work directly from you, without an agent you would still be at a disadvantage. As I mentioned in Chapter Four, these publishers have any number of divisions and each division has any number of its own imprints. Which ones to submit to? Your agent knows, or should know.

AGENTS HELP CLEAR THE MAZE

In addition to scads of divisions and imprints, each of these has its own roster of editors: e.g. editors responsible for romance novels only or editors responsible for historical novels only or editors who will look at nothing but mysteries.

Then we have editors who want to see two or three or even four different genres and editors who are interested only in nonfiction, but not all nonfiction.

Editor A wants to see memoirs, biographies and auto-biographies, but Editor B looks only at scientific works. Then, of course, there's the children's editor. I think you get the picture. Your agent should know which is which, and which one to send your query to.

AGENT/PUBLISHER RELATIONSHIP

Even more important, your agent has personal contacts with a variety of editors.

An experienced agent can pick up the phone and call Editor C and say, "Hi, Carolyn, I have a great one for you today. It just came in." Could you do that?

And not just with Editor C, your agent has a 'rolodex', computer, brain, filled with phone numbers of editors waiting for her call.

Well, maybe not waiting? But perhaps *willing* to take her call may be a more accurate description. Editors know that without agents they would have to scramble through huge slush piles of unsolicited manuscripts and they don't want to do that. So they view agents they are used to dealing with as reliable 'screeners' and give those agents a clearer path than you would receive as an un-agented author.

A good agent has earned the respect of editors who know they can depend on her to submit only the best material to them and to submit only material within their field of expertise.

For example, I mentioned McBooks Press in Chapter Four. My partner, Lois Bennett, sold a book to them that may not have gotten sold had she not been aware that they were looking for military material at that time. The book in question was a submarine themed thriller, which incidentally, went on to be listed on a "Best Thrillers of the Year" list.

AGENTS AS NEGOTIATORS

A good agent can sometimes obtain a better advance for her client than that which the publisher at first offers. Publishers are reluctant to offer large advances to first time, untried writers. I can remember times when we managed to jiggle the sum up a thousand or two. It's not always possible, but certainly an agent has a better chance of budging a budget-conscious editor than an independent writer.

AGENT/AUTHOR RELATIONSHIP

Having an agent can, and almost always will, help you develop your craft as a writer. If an agent sees real potential in your work, she will offer suggestions which will help you stretch that potential to its farthest point. She will guide you in ways which will help you avoid some of the pitfalls awaiting beginning writers.

You can also expect your agent to keep you informed of where he has submitted your query package and what responses he has received.

A good agent should provide this information in a timely manner so before you sign a contract with an agent, though you may be eager, ask him how often you can expect to hear from him. And If later he frequently fails to stick to his word to keep you informed, it's okay to check with him and remind him of his commitment. Communications is a vital part of the author/agent relationship.

On the other hand, remember that you are not your agent's only client. Remember that the major job of an agent is to sell your work and the work of his other clients to publishers. He can't do that if he is constantly on the telephone with you or constantly answering your e-mails. Yes, contact him if he is outrageously lax in reporting replies he has received from editors to you, but do not pester him. Let him do his work. It will benefit both of you. Remember an agent who sells other clients has a better chance of selling you.

Your agent will try to negotiate the best contract she possibly can for you. She will explain the small print and she will guide you through the signing process. This does not mean you don't have to engage an attorney to look at your contracts before you sign them—both the contract you will sign with your agent and the contract you will sign with the publisher. As we said earlier, you owe it to yourself, even if you have an agent, lawyer, or publisher 'friend', to fully understand what you are signing.

Having led you through the contract stage, your agent will be the referee between you and your editor, if you have a disagreement regarding something in your manuscript. She may not be able to settle all disputes, but she will want to help.

Lastly and, perhaps most importantly, she will hold your hand. When she has sent your "baby" to three different editors and received three different rejections; when you read in the paper that a first time writer has just signed a multi-book contract and you're still waiting; when you've signed a contract, but the editor wants you to change a section that is dear to your heart; when your friends are getting tired of hearing you moan about it; for any of these reasons and a dozen others, your agent will be there for you. She will commiserate with you and keep up your morale.

But, don't take advantage—remember her main job is selling your book! Do everything you can to support her, but always be alert that she is supporting you.

Most authors would kill for an agent. Some say it is tougher to get an agent than a publisher. Be that as it may, as in any other business, it is your responsibility to know whether an agent is all they say they are. But how do you know before you sign your so sought after agent contract? You need to know what a reputable agent should not do.

WHAT AN AGENT SHOULD NOT DO

An agent should not charge you one penny, with one possible exception of a few—very few—legitimate expenses, which I'll discuss shortly.

An agent should not charge you a reading fee or an editing fee. If he or she suggests doing so, run. Reputable agents do not charge fees for reading your work.

If you want someone to read through your manuscript and give you feedback in exchange for a fee, or if you want a line or a content editor to improve your manuscript—again for a fee—before you send it to the agent, fine. These 'for hire' editors fill an important niche in the publishing industry, however, they are independent of agents. While an agent may send you a list of editors to help you choose an independent editor, to offer that service himself for a fee is unethical in my opinion.

LEGITIMATE AGENT EXPENSES

We mentioned before that there are certain legitimate expenses an agent may charge an author. Two examples are postage and copying charges. Almost all small agencies pass these charges along to their clients, however, the postage charge should be only for the actual amount of postage it has cost the agent to send your materials to the editor, and the copy charge should be solely for your benefit. Be sure you have the amount of copying charges stated in your contract— so much per page for copying the manuscript to send to editors. I've heard some horror stories from writers who failed to have this in writing. In this case, do sweat the small stuff! Nobody likes expensive surprise fees.

In today's electronic world, these charges may become less and less a problem because manuscripts will more often be sent as e-mail attachments. In a short time when this expense is eliminated, an agent in an agency of any size should charge you absolutely zero postage and copying fees for handling your book.

So When Do I Get Paid?

In most agent agreements, the author designates the agent as the recipient for the advance and royalties paid by the publisher. The agent takes their agreed upon percentage and pre-agreed upon expenses and promptly sends a check for the balance to the author. *They* will pay *you* when they have successfully placed your book and a contract has been signed with a publishing house. This allows the agent to help you keep track of your income and expenses and gives you more time to do the other things needed to make your book and you successful.

THE SEARCH FOR AN AGENT

How do you begin your search for an agent? Three books which will assist in this search are:

* *Writer's Market*
* *Jeff Herman's Guide to Book Publishers, Editors & Literary Agents*
* *Guide to Literary Agents*

KEEP UP TO DATE

All three of these books are updated yearly. Be sure you have the current year's copy. There are many changes daily in the world of publishing. Houses open and close, editors and agents change companies and move. While agents don't move around as often as editors do, they do move from one agency to another on occasion, and agencies come and go. So you also will need to check on the agencies themselves. So be sure you have the latest versions of these books and recheck your information on the specific agent/company websites before you submit.

Here's another reason to stay up to date.

Let me say here (and I'll repeat it from time to time throughout the book), it is important to address any correspondence, whether it is electronic or via regular mail service, directly to an individual.

For example: Do not write: Dear Agent, or To Whom it May Concern.

Instead:
Take the time to determine the name of the person with whom you wish to correspond and be sure it is correctly spelled. And please, oh please, send it to the person to whom it is intended.

I can't tell you how many times I received correspondence addressed to another agent, but I can tell you without reservation, that this sort of carelessness turns an agent or editor off before they even open your envelope. When it happens to me, I promptly delete the e-mail, or put the letter into the round file. Agents and publishers are too busy to deal with amateurs and carelessness.

Getting back to the resource books:

The Guide to Literary Agents is exactly what it claims to be, a listing of agents only. It is invaluable since it also gives you other useful information such as a list of agents who are interested in seeing scripts, and a list of writers' conferences, a great way to meet an agent.

Both *Writer's Market* and *Jeff Herman's Guide* list agents, but go beyond, listing book and magazine publishers and providing a wealth of information to help new writers: e.g. tips on query letters, how to build a platform, and using social media. (Chapter Fifteen) Very helpful too is a list of the conferences members of the agency attend.

The listings may also tell you the percentage of new to unpublished writers the agency represents. The greater percentage of new writers, the greater your odds of acceptance, it seems to me. But don't mark agencies with low percentages of first time writers off your list entirely. You don't want to miss any bets. As long as an agency publishes some beginners, don't ignore them, just put them toward the bottom of your list and approach those who seem more welcoming to newbies first.

Listings will also give you the titles of the most recent books the agency has sold. This reinforces the information the agency has displayed on their website in regard to the types of material they handle. It wastes your time and the agent's time when you send inappropriate material so check this out carefully and save everyone, including yourself, valuable time and effort.

Other information included in these directories may regard contracts. You'll learn whether a contract is offered, the length of the contract and the terms, such as the percentages of the sale price charged as commissions they keep for domestic and foreign sales.

Each of these resource books has its own set of plusses and minuses so take a trip to your local bookstore or library and examine all three to decide which is best for you

Once you have chosen your favorite directory, take some time to study the entries. Look closely and make a list of a few agencies that handle the kind of writing you do.

If you write nonfiction, it might be best to select a few agencies which focus on nonfiction only, but throw a couple in the mix that handle both nonfiction and fiction if you write both. The same is true if you write fiction. This may provide you the ability to use the same agent if you decide to write in another genre.

Don't stop there! Check out what types of fiction and nonfiction the agencies handle specifically.

For example:
In their listing in the 2011 Edition of *Writer's Market*, the Elaine P. English Literary Agency states that they represent novels, so you wouldn't send them a nonfiction work. Further, the agency lists the specific fiction areas in which they are interested. They go a step further and tell you which areas they are currently actively seeking and, equally important, they tell you the types of fiction they do not want to receive—all excellent information to have before you submit.

Another example:
Conversely, in the same resource book, Linden Publishing, Inc. wants nonfiction only. They list the types of nonfiction they publish, tell you exactly what to submit and let you know that they prefer electronic files.

It's so important for you to pay attention to the information in these agent listings.

For example, do not under any circumstances send a manuscript for a thriller to an agent who specifies that she doesn't want thrillers. You are fighting a lost cause. *You* may think your thriller is so good that once she reads it, she will be willing to represent it. *But she has already told you she isn't* going to read it. And worse yet, this agent will mentally assign 'amateur' status to you and think you must be a little 'thick' to so blatantly ignore what has been clearly stated. Forget about future submissions to this agent.

Finally, these valuable listings often contain "Tips" from the agents and agencies. Read and heed!

HOW DO I KNOW IF AN AGENT IS ETHICAL

It is difficult to get an agent, and authors celebrate when they receive an agent contract, but some live to regret it. How can you know the agent is ethical?

AAR is the acronym for Association of Authors' Representatives, a prestigious organization for literary agents. If an agent has the initials AAR following his name, you can be sure that he will not charge you for reading, critiquing or editing. He will follow the ethical procedures set out by the organization.

Does this mean you should approach only agents who are AAR?

Not at all. For one reason or another, an agent may not belong to the organization. It may be a new agency or one that has not yet sold the requisite number of books to qualify for membership. The membership fee is quite stiff, therefore, the agency may be well established, but not want to pay the fee on general principles. Being an AAR member is just one indication that an agent is legitimate, but does not guarantee that an agent will fulfill his responsibilities. You have to do that by due diligence.

CONFERENCES: GREAT PLACES TO MEET AGENTS

Attending a conference is an excellent place to contact an agent. Before, or after you make your reservation for a conference, you will receive a copy of the program. Look at the names and bios of the agents who will be attending and note who will be scheduling brief interviews with authors. Of special interest may be those who are presenting since you will be able to get a preview of their communication ability and knowledge of their subject area. Immediately, request to be put on his or her schedule if you like what you see and read.

"Immediately" is the operative word here.
The ratio of agents to writers at any conference is lopsided. Almost every writer attending will want to talk to the agents. These coveted spots fill up quickly, so you must get your request in early. Check out the specific agent's website and blog to get a better picture of their interests and how you will relate with them.

BE PREPARED!!!

Arrive at the conference armed with copies of your work and, most important, know exactly what your "pitch" will be. Your time with the agent will be short so you want to take the best possible advantage of every minute.

Have extra copies of your manuscript with you, especially the first few chapters. You never know, an agent just might ask for a copy then and there. (Many agents, traveling, may provide special mailing instructions since they are limited in what they can transport so don't be discouraged if they do not accept your submission package.)

Author Olive Church says that in the beginning of her career one of the steps she took in her attempt to be represented by an agent was attending conferences in order to meet them. "I followed everybody's tips and made up new ones as I went along. The best way to get a good agent to agree to represent you is to meet her in person." She adds, "It also helps, if you can get an established writer to recommend you to her agent!"

DO YOU NEED AN AGENT?

This is a very common question so let's examine it carefully.

As noted at the beginning of this chapter, there are any number of ways in which an agent can be helpful to a writer, the primary one being the ability to submit your material to a major publishing house closed to un-agented writers. Now, let's look at the down side of this service.

THE NEGATIVES

Having read this far into the chapter, you are aware of the time and effort you must put into finding an agent who will agree to represent your book. With the numbers of as yet unpublished writers, and established authors, clamoring for representation, your chances are slim at best.

Even if an agent does accept your manuscript, after months of waiting for a response, there is no guarantee she will be able to place it with a major house. If she places it at all it may be with a smaller house, one that you could have approached yourself without the delay of submitting to an agent.

The real questions you must ask are:

- Do you want to expend the time and effort you must put into this search in view of the slim chances for success?
- Do you want to spend the money for postage and copies if that expenditure will net you nothing?
- If you do find an agent who will work for you, do you want to sit around waiting for her to place a work that she may not in the end succeed in placing?

It's pleasant to have someone with whom you can bounce ideas around and to hold your hand when a rejection arrives or to suggest how you might improve the manuscript.

It's certainly fun to drop the phrase, "My agent..." into your conversations, especially those with other writers. Having an agent lends a writer a certain prestige. But is it worth all the trouble you've gone through when at the end most people find themselves right back where they started?

Yes, some new authors do land an agent, so I don't want to discourage you. But why not spend that time, money and effort on placing your first novel yourself?

You've researched the resource books mentioned in Chapters Seventeen and the Appendix. You know the many mid-sized and small presses that are available and interested in your type of writing. Why not focus on them? Choose a group of these publishers and begin submitting to them, but first, read Chapter Nine and Ten.

Now you know the arguments on both sides of the agent issue and can make an educated decision on whether not to devote your time, energy and money to attract an agent. Whatever decision you have made—to promote your book directly to publishers yourself, or to try to find an agent who will represent your book to the major publishing houses—go for it! And good luck!

THERE IS ANOTHER WAY

On the other hand, if you have decided you would rather put your efforts into getting the book published, on the market quickly, study the self-publishing chapter (Chapter Twelve) carefully. This may be the route for you.

CHAPTER SEVEN

WHAT DO EDITORS DO

TYPES OF EDITORS

It's easy to confuse the different types of editors.

Throughout this book I've used the generic term "editor" for various types of editors. The English language is confusing at best. It might seem that in this instance it could be made less confusing simply by always referring to a *line editor* or a *content editor*, sometimes called a *developmental editor*. Unfortunately, it gets complicated.

For starters, some editors function as both. Others hire themselves out as freelance or independent editors, who will perform one or both of these functions for a fee. Editors who work for a publishing house perform the same services, but receive their compensation from the publisher. Once a writer has had his material accepted by the publisher, the in-house editing is free to him.

So let's clear this up a bit so you know what editors do to help you.

LINE EDITORS

A line editor looks for and corrects mistakes in such areas as punctuation, spelling, typos and grammar. She does this line-by-line, explaining her title. All writers should have their work checked by an independent line editor. Especially writers like me, who tend to rush our work.

Line editors can be a big help to the finished work:

They know things the typical author may not. The 'Grammar Granny', a.k.a. Martha Jeffers, once told me that every semicolon, colon, comma or apostrophe needs a reason for its existence. "'Because that's the way I talk,' doesn't cut it," she said.

As for my writing, she informed me that I use commas "as if they're sprinkled from a salt shaker."

I expect that way back when I went to school, the rules differed substantially from those of today. At a recent discussion, writer and poet, Allen Watson said, "The rules for commas have changed. Fewer and fewer commas are used these days." Times change and so does writing preferences.

It's a question that can raise hackles on either side of the argument. Some argue that a comma should be placed wherever there would be a pause in conversation or when reading the piece aloud. Others would use commas to set apart any phrase not necessary to the meaning of the sentence. For example, "She took the bouquet, still wrapped in shiny paper, and the champagne into the kitchen." Some university dissertation editors are adamant that a semi-colon must precede the use of "however," which then must be followed by a comma. I think you get the picture.

The line editor is someone who must keep up with current usage so things like comma usage in your manuscript is something that your line editor will determine so you can be creative.

Quality editing is important, so as with anything else we've discussed, you need references before you hire anyone. I've seen some material that looked as if it had been edited by an orangutan. An experience of mine some years ago wasn't quite that bad, but it was nerve wracking.

My doctoral dissertation was in the hands of an excellent typist, but when she passed the sections on to my editor, said editor proceeded to change much of the punctuation. The typist retyped it and submitted it to the dissertation committee who then threw it back to her changing the punctuation back to the way she had done it in the first place before the woman who called herself an editor had gotten her hands on it.

So, with those words of warning, a line editor is worth her fee as long as she knows what she's doing. And As with any other service, check with a few prior clients before committing your work.

CONTENT EDITORS AKA DEVELOPMENT EDITORS

As the title suggests, a content editor deals with the content of the manuscript, "develops" it. Sometimes the changes they want to make can be surprising to the neophyte and the experienced author. The newer you are, the less control you may have.

One shocker may be that the CE may cut the entire first chapter. Why would he do that?

Many first time writers use the first chapter for background material that either isn't necessary for the story or which can be interspersed later in the manuscript. Often the action of a novel doesn't begin until the second chapter rather than the first.

He might also move content around or cut here and there or ask you to expand an area.

An example of this occurred when the content editor I had hired to edit my first novel returned the copy to me. The margins beside the paragraphs were filled with the notation: *This should be a scene*. What did she mean?

In single paragraphs, I had "told" information that needed to be "shown" as a scene. Once I understood this, I followed her suggestions, paragraphs becoming pages. The book expanded to a better length and became a much more interesting read. The content author often sees things we as authors may be too close to our work to see.

More recently, I acted as a content editor for one of the writers whose book I published. It was a great book. The writer had an excellent platform (more about that in Chapter Fifteen), and had written a fast moving suspenseful thriller, but he had over-filled the pages with unnecessary material. I cut whole chapters. The final product proved to be the best-selling book I've published.

As with a line editor, a content editor has to know his stuff. Check him out before you sign.

IN HOUSE EDITORS

You've submitted your material. It's been accepted and you've signed a contract. Now the work with your house editor begins. This will ideally be the second or third editor who will look at your work because before you've ever submitted it to an agent, or a publisher, you will have had it edited by a line editor, a content editor, or both of your choosing. You want to submit the best manuscript possible.

The in-house editor is assigned to you by your publisher to catch any problems the other editors might have missed, to help you make the book conform to what the publisher is looking for in his books.

Please listen carefully and with an open mind. She is an expert on these things. She knows what the reading public is looking for. She knows what kind of titles will help to promote the book and which will hinder sales, just as the cover designer knows what will attract a potential customer to pick the book up for a closer look. The person responsible for the blurbs on the cover knows what will entice the prospective reader to buy the book once the cover has encouraged him to pick it up in the first place.

The in-house editor, an employee of the publisher, who works in concert with others in the publication house, may—you shudder to think—actually want to change the title of your work! This beautiful title you agonized over for days is now being pushed aside.

But it's your book. You wrote it.

That's exactly the point. You are a **writer**. The publishing house hires marketing people to work with your finished product. You are the expert on your book. They are the experts on what will sell your book.

Let's look at some examples.

The cover is the first thing a prospective purchaser sees. If the cover appeals to her, she will look further at your book. She will turn the book over and read the back cover. Your publisher has marketing experts who will compose and arrange the material used in this vital component of your book. Tell your editor your concerns. Tell him why you think your cover or title is perfect for the book and then let go. Don't fight them. Remember, they want the book to be successful as much as you do.

Work with your in-house editor. At this point, she is your best friend. If you disagree with her, you can take a stand on principle. Or you can remember what happened to the writer mentioned in Chapter Four, who thought someone else would take his manuscript. It's your choice, but make sure you understand what you are risking.

Finally, and it may take some time, and some give-and-take, you and your in-house editor have agreed upon the finished content of the book and it goes to press. All the little battles will seem just that when you have your book launch party and the next day you wake up and realize you are a published author. With the help of your editors, you've achieved the dream of every writer.

I sincerely hope it becomes a reality for you. So does your publisher. And that is important to always remember: your publisher wants you to succeed!!!

ACQUISITIONS EDITORS

An acquisitions editor functions much the same as an agent does as far as reading and evaluating your submission and making a decision about its potential. These are the editors, employees of the publisher, who evaluate the query packages you send to those publishing houses that will accept material directly from you, the author.

Some acquisitions editors perform this function full time, while for others, especially heads of small publishing houses—people like Carole Stuart at Barricade Books or Leanne Burroughs at Highland Press—it's one job of many.

Everything we discussed in Chapter Six about literary agents applies to the work of acquisition editors.

EDITORS ARE HUMAN

While there will be times when you will have your doubts, agents and editors are people too. Treat them with courtesy and respect for what they do and your life with these professionals, who are absolutely indispensable to the success of your work, will be mutually rewarding. They will want to do a good job for you.

WHAT'S NEXT?

We've talked about agents and the different types of editors. In the next chapter, we'll back up a bit and talk about how to deal with agents and editors in general. What they might expect from you, and what you can expect from them. Read on!

CHAPTER EIGHT

HOW TO CONTACT AND WORK WITH AN EDITOR OR AGENT

You've done your homework. You've selected an agent or several agents or editors at publishing houses that don't require agented submissions. You think your book would be a good fit with these agents and editors. Now, you must make contact with them. As we all know, a first impression can often be a deal killer. Don't let this happen to you.

THE KEY TO CONTACTING AN AGENT/EDITOR

The relevant message here is: Be professional. For example, don't indulge in gimmicks. You may have heard someone say that sending your manuscript in a pizza box will insure it will break out from the pack—get it noticed—make an impact?

That is correct. It will make an impact— unfortunately, a negative one.

Few approaches irritate an agent or an editor more than receiving unprofessional gimmicks. At worse, it will result in your precious manuscript being dumped in the nearest trash container. At best, it will result in one large strike against it when (and if) the agent or editor reluctantly reviews it.

I once received an eighteen-inch stuffed toy alligator which, when squeezed, sang the song: "Alligator, Alligator." I did not offer representation to the author, who apparently thought such a presentation was "cute." The toy may be cute, but it is the manuscript that sells the book, not the distractions.

Agents and editors agree that they want to connect with writers who treat every aspect of their craft with respect. So to make the best impression on an agent or an editor, follow the procedures of the professionals.

The information I'm going to give you in these chapters isn't absolute for all situations. You will find variations in the expectations of various agents and editors, but generally, if you follow these suggestions, they will keep you from looking like an amateur and, hopefully, will put you ahead of the game. For that reason, this chapter and the two to follow may be the most important of the entire book to some of you. Although I think the whole book is important.

Unless you are meeting an agent or an editor at a conference (covered in Chapter Six) your approach will be by e-mail or snail mail.

Email/Snail Mail Contact Tips

The first rule never to be deviated from in contacting any agent or editor is *always research fully* before attempting contact.

Look agent/editor listings up in one of the resource books I have discussed. Make notes regarding how she wants to be approached: via a web site online; e-mail; or via old-fashioned but the easy to use, United States Postal Service.

If she requests e-mail, be sure you know whether she wants the material in the body of the e-mail or if she will accept attachments. More and more people in the industry have moved into electronic messaging, but find out if the person to whom you are applying prefers this method by visiting their website.

If your recipient does not state they accept email, you must assume they want you to use the regular mail. What you should send and how are covered in the next two chapters.

Also important: Don't telephone a query to either an agent or an editor. Call her office to confirm a name or an address if you must, but not to ask if she will represent or is interested in publishing your book.
Recently I received a message on my machine that went like this:

"Um, I'm um (and he gave his name), um I'm an author and um, I wrote a book. I'd uh like to get it published. Um, would you be uh interested?" The caller um'ed and uh'ed a bit more before stating his telephone number. Like this gentlemen, most people will do a better job of selling their project through the accepted channels of communications and leaving a phone message pitch about your book, even if you don't "um", isn't very effective.

So even though I'm sure that every writer reading this book is capable of making an intelligent telephone call, don't. Phone calls may be acceptable for following up submission after a reasonable amount of time, but not for submitting your work.

HOW AGENTS RESPOND

You've now made contact with an agent or editor of your choice. You've sent off the appropriate material in an acceptable, professional, manner. Now you wait—but for how long?

Waiting can be frustrating unless you understand the process.

Generally speaking, you can expect to receive a response within a reasonable time—a month to six weeks. That is dependent, of course, on your having submitted in the proper form. If not, you may get it back immediately, or you may never get it back. Many agencies today specify they do not return manuscripts nor reply to submissions unless they are interested in pursuing them further. It is a very competitive and busy profession with little time for what the writer may feel is minimal courtesy, but would make the job even more cumbersome than it is.

Response time is also dependent on the specific agent or editor. Lois Bennett and I always tried to respond as quickly as possible. That may have been because we are both writers and have firsthand knowledge of the stress of waiting to find out if we've struck out or are going to be accepted. Even years later, when I think of it, I can still experience the excitement I felt when an agent sent me a letter of acceptance for my first novel. I would hope other agents/editors try their best as well to respond as they would want to have their submissions responded to.

You will find many agents and editors who do respond quickly. Unfortunately, there are those who do not. Don't try to read anything into this. Just as a fast response can mean a rejection, it can also mean an acceptance and vice versa. It can mean that your work is under consideration or it can mean that the agent or editor is trying to find her way out from under the hundreds and hundreds of queries she receives. Or it could mean that she is disorganized and hasn't gotten around to your work, or it could (but seldom does) mean that it has been lost—not if you have your name on every page and have every page numbered as you always should do.

So, what do you do when a couple of months go by and you still haven't received any word about your query package, even though you were careful to include your e-mail address or a self-addressed, stamped envelope (SASE), as requested?

It is acceptable now to telephone and to say politely that you sent a query package on such-and-such a date and you are checking to be sure she received it.

What you do *not* want to do is to call or write in anger, wanting to know what she has done with your manuscript.

Chances are the agent/editor hasn't been careless. Chances are she has a backlog and may not have a system built in by the agency/publisher to notify writers of the delays. Or the delay may mean she really is reviewing it for possible acceptance, but needs more time. If you are impolite at this point, the agent or editor may decide she doesn't want to tie herself up with a writer who can't control his temper, or doesn't have knowledge of the process.

But let's say you do receive a response three or four weeks after you have mailed your query. It will arrive usually in one of three ways:
- a form letter of rejection
- a personal letter of rejection
- a letter requesting you to send your entire manuscript.

Nobody likes form letters or rejections, but don't take it personally. The reasons for rejecting a work frequently have nothing to do with the quality of writing. It may be that the book doesn't fit their list or needs at this time, or that they already have a book similar to yours, or they may have budget issues. Keep on trying.

A personal letter, even a rejection, is in itself an achievement. Congratulations, the agent has seen something in your writing that she likes and she's taken the time from her busy schedule to tell you so. If you receive comments and suggestions with your rejection, consider them carefully before you resubmit to this agent/editor, or another. In some very rare cases, the agent may invite you to resubmit with the suggested changes to their agency and that is something you should seriously consider. It is however, not a guarantee that even with the changes, this agent or editor will accept you.

Finally, if you receive a request for your entire manuscript, I congratulate you again. This is the best response yet; however, after a mini celebration, settle down. Unfortunately, you're not home yet. It's a giant step in the right direction but not the offer of a contract.

In Chapter Eleven, I'll discuss rejection letters in detail. For the moment, let's imagine that you receive one of the following responses and see how you should proceed.

You receive an e-mail or letter requesting you send your entire manuscript:

You've moved up to the second level but I hate to bust your balloon, agents and editors ask for many more complete manuscripts from authors than they can offer contracts for representation. Follow through by sending the manuscript concisely following her instructions or the guidelines in Chapter Ten of this book. Include a short note of thanks in your package, but just that. Keep it short. Say thanks and stop.

You receive a contract:

FROM AN AGENT:
Congratulations! Now you really can celebrate. But what about thanking your agent or editor? Even if she has telephoned to tell you the news, and you have verbally thanked her, send her a short note of thanks anyway.

After an agent accepts you, always treat her with respect, and remember she still has a lot of work to do for you and her other clients. Don't inundate her with phone calls or e-mails. Her job now is to sell your book to a publisher. Remember that you are not her only client. If your agent is going to spend her time contacting publishers, time is precious. She won't have time to do her job successfully if you and her other clients keep her on the phone or keep her busy responding to your e-mails. On the other hand, respond to her questions and requests promptly and completely and steer clear to let her do her job.

FROM AN EDITOR/PUBLISHER

If the contract you have received is from an editor—a contract to publish your book—much the same advice holds. The service she is providing for you differs here from that of the agent, but she also is extremely busy. She will give you all the time you need to make your book the best it can be, but understand that she has other duties also. You build good will when you understand what these professionals must do to make your book, and other books, successful.

Your initial approach to an agent or editor can set the tone for your future. Hopefully, it will be a long and mutually beneficial relationship, so you'll want it to be as positive as possible.

COMING UP NEXT

We now know who to submit to and how they may respond. We also have a clearer understanding of the roles many professionals play in making our books successful. You can help yourself and prospective agents and publishers by knowing exactly what materials to send to them. Read on!

CHAPTER NINE

HOW TO PREPARE A QUERY PACKAGE FOR FICTION

Much of the information in this and the following two chapters has been adapted from my earlier book, *An Agent Speaks: A Primer for Unpublished Writers*. What I wrote then applies even more so today. With the advent of POD publishers (Print/publish on Demand—see Chapter Twelve) and the greater access to publishing opportunities, the competition to become published and successfully market your book has grown dramatically.

In the introduction to that book, I explained I became a literary agent because I believed unpublished writers needed more agents who would give them the same attention as they give to established writers. Unfortunately, I soon realized that most of these writers are not aware of the formula for submitting manuscripts, a formula that, when ignored, tags the writer as an amateur. I noted that no matter how good your manuscript is, it won't get published if neither an agent nor an editor reads it, and they won't read it unless it conforms to professional standards.

At least seventy-five percent of the material arriving in my office was lacking in several important areas. The same holds true for the queries arriving today in my small press publishing house. A poorly prepared query package can doom a good manuscript before it ever has a chance at publication.

If you think this doesn't apply to you because you have a carefully typed manuscript with carefully selected fonts for the various headings and everything is packaged beautifully in a professional folder, you're wrong. I feel badly for those writers who try so hard, but for lack of the proper information, come off looking like amateurs when a little knowledge and careful preparation can give them the edge they need. So let's discuss the nitty-gritty of these critical elements to your successful submission.

RULE #1

Before reading another line, Rule Number One for writing query letters is:

***Don't write that letter* if you haven't completely finished your novel.**

Neither an agent nor an editor should be approached in regard to a work of fiction until the last "i" has been dotted and the last "t" crossed. You may well have been checking out agents or editors in advance, but don't even think of approaching one until your manuscript is finished, proof read and polished to the best shine possible. Once that's completed, And don't write that letter until you read the next sections carefully.

HOW TO FORMULATE YOUR MANUSCRIPT

Most of this information should be common sense, but some— use of fancy fonts, packaging, copyright— may be a surprise and could doom your submission to the 'never-heard-from-again' slush pile.

RULE #2

Queries and manuscripts must be typed.

This may appear to be a given, but I have received more than one handwritten query. I can only suppose the manuscript would have been handwritten also—that is if I had been foolish enough to request a copy. Most agents/editors will not.

As with anything else, exceptions occur, such as the query I received from a prisoner without access even to a typewriter, much less a computer. Based on his circumstances, I read the query, but unfortunately, the content was as poor as his handwriting.

Here are some of the common elements you need to know to format your submission.

Font: Style and size of type

This is not a time to impress with your unique typing style. Do not use fancy fonts. Use 12 point Times New Roman or Courier New throughout. (I prefer Times New Roman.) Do not type chapter identifications or titles in larger point. Leave that to the individual who will design the layout of the book at the publishing house. Your aim is to present a clean, easily readable manuscript and not one with distractions.

Spacing and formatting
Query letters/synopses

You should always single space for query letters and synopses, flush left (block paragraphs). Use double spacing only between paragraphs.

Manuscripts

Manuscripts should be double spaced, with the first sentence of each paragraph indented. Double spacing allows for edit marks and comments. And, yes, your "perfect" manuscript is going to need some editing.

You should double-double space between scenes. Do not use stars (***) to indicate scene or time changes.

Begin your introduction, prologue and chapters one-quarter to one-third down the page. Be consistent. Begin each chapter on a new page.

Identification:
Place a header at the top of every manuscript page.
(This function can be performed automatically by your computer once you set it).

Your specific header will consist of your last name, slash, the title of your book, or if the title is a long one, a key word or words from the title.

For example, the alternating headers for this book were:

How to Sell Your Books: A Publisher Speaks, and *Joan West*

I am constantly astonished by the number of submissions I receive with no author identification on the pages. Surprisingly, this omission is not confined to first-time writers. Many writers who should know better are guilty of this obvious omission which makes it difficult to identify their work.

With the number of manuscripts and chapters floating around an agent's or an editor's office at any given time, it is imperative that each page include identification. If ever an agent has lost your manuscript, and it happens—rarely—but it does happen, ask yourself if you had identified the pages before you call and blame her.

This caution holds for any other material you send: be sure to have identifying information on all letters, synopses, author biographies, anything—everything. It may take a little time, but boy it can save a lot more.

Page Numbers:
Page numbers are placed in the upper right-hand corner of every page. Your computer should perform this function automatically once you insert the header. Use the numeral

only. Do not choose the "Page 1" option or any other; numeral only.

Note: On the printed book, the page numbers may appear in a different position than in your submission. That's because the book designer put them there to enhance the design. On the manuscript, they always belong in that upper right-hand corner to keep things uniform and simple.

Word Count:
Type the word count in the upper left-hand corner of the first page of the manuscript.

You can obtain the word count as a function on your computer.

The header is already in the upper left-hand corner, you may be thinking? Yes, but the header and the page number, both of which were attached by your computer, are higher on the page, outside the typing area.

Be sure you state the word count, as opposed to the page count. The number of pages will change according to other variables: font type and size, page size, book design.

Cover Sheet:
You should include a cover sheet along with the sample chapters and your query, or with your manuscript, when it is requested.

Type the title of the book, its genre and word count and all of your contact information on the cover sheet: name, address, e-mail address, web site, land line telephone number and cell phone number. Do not add any extraneous matter. Only this important information should be printed clearly on the cover sheet.

E-mail:

We discussed this earlier, but it bears repeating. Only some agencies and publishing houses prefer to receive e-mail queries; some don't. Be sure you know which ones are which before you query. If they do not specifically state they accept E-mail queries, play it safe and snail-mail.

Proofread:

Proofread everything: letters, bio, manuscript and synopses. Have one or two friends, writing colleagues proofread. If possible have a freelance editor proof it too. You have one shot at demonstrating your commitment and professionalism, so proofread, proofread, proofread.

THOSE ARE THE DO'S ---NOW FOR THE DON'TS:

PACKAGING

1.Do not package your material in any fancy way. Agents/Editors want it easy to get to.

You may paperclip your query letter, synopsis, marketing plan and writer's biography together if you are sending all of these items.

Place your chapters and/or manuscript loosely in an envelope or manuscript box.

2. **Do not put your manuscript in a folder** of any kind. Above all else, do not put your manuscript in a three-ring binder. Use no folders, fancy or otherwise. If this requirement will keep you awake nights, it is permissible to put a single rubber band around the chapters or manuscript—nothing else.

3. **When e-mailing a submission, do not send attachments** unless you have the permission of the agent.

4. Do not telephone. It probably won't do you any good anyway. Neither agents nor editors have time to drop everything and look for your material or its status.

5. **Do not put a copyright** notation anywhere in your submission. Huh?

Obtain a copyright if you must, but don't tell the agent or editor to whom you are sending it that it's copyrighted. Think about it. What's the main reason for obtaining the copyright? It's to prevent unscrupulous individuals from stealing your work, isn't it? So, what does that say to an agent when she removes the material from the envelope and sees Copyright 2012 staring at her? Believe me, it puts you at a disadvantage.

Those are the basic rules, the do's and do not's, of presenting your material for review. The procedures touched upon in this chapter are so important that many of them will be repeated and expanded in other chapters of the book.

These guidelines may vary slightly agency to agency, but only in minor ways. Your agent or editor may send you a set of guidelines for submitting to her. If so, follow them, of course. In fact, follow them to the letter. If she does not send guidelines, follow the ones presented in this chapter in order to make a good first impression with your presentation.

THE QUERY PACKAGE

With a properly formatted complete novel in manuscript form, you will now need to put together a query package.

Every query package will consist of:
- a query letter
- a synopsis
- a marketing plan
- a writer's biography/platform
- a portion of your manuscript

Let's take a look at what is needed for each of these component parts.

QUERY LETTER

The query letter is the first thing, other than the envelope, your prospective agent or publisher sees. It is also the first thing they will read to judge your abilities. It is how you first, and very concisely, present your book and yourself so it should be an example of your best writing.

THE HOOK
Most advice concerning query letters stresses the need for a "hook."

Hooks are of paramount importance in paragraph one, page one of your manuscript, and at the start of your query letter. In your book you want the reader to be so curious, so interested, he can't wait to turn to page two. While no page two exists in a query letter, it is equally important to entice an agent to want to read your manuscript. That hook in your first paragraph of your query letter will make him salivate to read your entire letter, packet and masterpiece.

DID I HEAR RIGHT? ONE PAGE?

Let's stop right here and repeat: *"No page two exists in a query letter."* All the component parts of a query letter must be stated within the confines of one page.

I'm covering my ears to drown out your shouts of protest. But, yes, it's not only possible to limit a query letter to one page, it's imperative. You have one page to prove your book is worth the time and effort to continue.

It may take work, a lot of re-writes, a lot of thought and maneuvering, but trust me, you can do it. You have to, because a busy agent or editor will not turn the page. Even more important, she wants to know if you can "write tight." The query letter will give her a clue.

So what are the other necessary elements of a query letter?

AFTER THE HOOK

After the hook, you need to write a one or two paragraph synopsis of the content of your book. For obvious reasons, these will be short and concise, but keep the reader's interest in your project.

You will also need to include three essential bits of information: word count, genre and title.

These can all be included in one sentence: e.g. "My 76,000 word romantic suspense novel titled *The Broken Door...* " This sentence doesn't take up much space, but these three pieces of information are critical.

Word Count

The greatest hook in the world is not going to sell a 60,000 word manuscript to an agent who is looking for one of 90,000 words.

Well, maybe if the hook is so strong and you're a little closer together than that. Say your book is 65,000 words and she wants 75,000, she might wonder if maybe she can get you to add another 10,000 words. The point is that she needs to know your word count (not your page count), and if you fail to state it in your query letter, you will be faulted for the omission.

Genre

If you've done your homework, you won't send a YA (young adult) manuscript to an agent who handles only adult material. But, even if you know she handles the genre you are querying, she may handle more than one genre and needs to know which category yours fits into.

Title

Titles should be viewed as a first selling point of your book and you should take great care in selecting a title that accurately represents your subject matter. The publisher may want to change it, but she wants to know what you have called it as a way of knowing what it is she about to read. A good title should be interesting and offer a hint of what to expect.

Additional inclusions to your query are flexible, but remember your one page limit. But what might help you sell a book?

BLURBS Etc.

Suppose a famous person has offered to give you an endorsement that you can use as a cover blurb. You will want to include it. This is especially true if the famous person happens to be a writer who writes in the same genre that you do.

If you know someone on one of the national morning shows and he has offered to get you an appearance on the show that would be a grabber. Of course, even if the president of the United States offered you an endorsement, the book still has to be well-written, but it sure would help.

Speaking of endorsements, let me make a couple of points. Don't confuse your local book reviewer with a *Nationally known reviewer,* and your local television station is not CBS. Both local and national outlets have a place in your path to publication, and can be very helpful, but the local organizations don't belong in your query letter.

BIO INFORMATION
A query letter is not the place to tell your life story. You only have one page. Remember? Only include bio information that sells your book: e.g. awards for writing, relevant experience, credentials that may demonstrate expertise.

Do *not* include biographical information such as where you went to school, your marital state or the number of children you have.

Do *not* offer the information that you have been writing since you were in kindergarten, that you were the editor of your school publication—high school or college. The query letter is about your book—*not about you!*

No matter how interesting you are or your life has been, it won't sell your book if it isn't well-written. If you have room, it is admissible to add a sentence at the close of the letter saying something like: I live in San Francisco with my husband and three children.

The letter will conclude with a list of what you are sending and that will be whatever the agent has requested in his guidelines or what is included in the guidelines I have provided.

Don't become all flowery with "...thank you so much for giving me the privilege of sending my manuscript to you....." "Thank you" or "Sincerely yours" (leave out the "very") and your name is sufficient.

Once you have these essential points covered, you'll want to check out a couple of other items. For instance, and we've said it before, but it is so important to be sure to address your letter to the agent by name.

A call to the agency will give you not only the correct name, but the correct spelling. I shudder every time I open a query letter and find it addressed "To Whom it May Concern" or "Dear Sir or Madam." If you want me to respect your work, give me the courtesy of knowing my name. Second: If you haven't taken the trouble to find out my name, what else about your work have you not taken the time to do correctly?

HOOK OR OVER-USED?
To go back to the opening paragraph of your query for a moment, if you've heard that the best way to begin a query letter is to write: "What would happen if"—followed by the premise of your story, stop and think before you use it. I wish I had kept a record of how many times that tired line came across my desk or through my e-mail.

If you read that the best way to begin a query letter is such-and-such or this-and-that? *Don't!*

You can be sure hundreds or thousands of writers have read the same book and will begin their query letters the same way. You're a writer. Be inventive. Be imaginative. Be yourself. But be professional.

Yes, do be professional. I received a query letter which I dumped immediately, so I can't quote it verbatim, but it went something like this: "I'm looking for a lazy agent who is looking to get rich." If I told you it went downhill from there, you'd have a pretty good idea of the remainder.

BE PROFESSIONAL

Watch for the little things that can trip you up:
- spelling and grammar.
- Use exclamation marks sparingly, if at all.
- Focus, don't wander. Say it precisely.
- Don't criticize other authors, agents, publishers, anyone.
- Don't praise yourself or your book.
- Don't say that your friends, family, students love your book.
- Don't mention money.
- Don't make personal comments.

In other words, once again and forever: Be professional.

THE SYNOPSIS

You've written a one page query letter. Here comes "writing tight" again. Now you must write a one page synopsis, which includes the beginning, middle and end of your story. Yes, the ending. Do not keep the conclusion a secret from the agent. Your big surprise ending cannot be a surprise for the people considering representing or publishing it. Maybe *you* already know this, but you'd be amazed how many wannabe writers do not. I can attest to that. More than one writer has sent me a synopsis ending with, "Read my manuscript to learn the big surprise." Agents/editors don't want to be surprised, they need to know.

You may be asked for a lengthier, more detailed, version or you may be asked for a chapter-by-chapter synopsis. It's always a good idea to write the chapter synopsis for your own benefit, even if it isn't required by the agents you have contacted. It helps to clarify the book for you.

A rule-of-thumb for a chapter-by-chapter synopsis is a sentence for every page in the chapter. This is flexible, but remember conciseness is appreciated.

YOUR MARKET PLAN

Today, even the larger houses, those that require an agented submission, will want to see a market plan that tells them what part you are willing to play to sell your book. And every author is expected to take an active role in what is a cooperative effort so a plan is expected and something you need to think about at every stage of your writing/publishing process.

What does a market plan consist of? The elements within any given plan can have many variations depending significantly on the personality of the writer and the specifications of the agent/publisher.
Most plans include the standard promotions:
- book signings
- appearances on local television and radio
- articles that you solicit from local newspapers or newsletters
- articles you write for various outlets; your blog; your web site
- presentations you will make
- events you will attend
- whatever you plan to do to promote the sales of your book.

You will be expected to develop a plan that is unique to you, and your book, or situation. Look for what and who you know that are related to your subject.

If your book is about airplanes, you might write articles for publications that cater to airplanes, trade magazines or airline magazines, for example.

If your book is about any type of animal, you might want to partner with a local veterinarian or shelter.

One of my clients was an attorney. He belonged to several legal associations each of which published its own newsletter. He committed to posting a notice in each. This is another area in which you can let your imagination soar.

An excellent market plan will do more than keep you on track with your public relations and letting the agent or editor know how committed you are to joining in the push to sell your book. It might be the factor that give you the 'edge':

Suppose an editor likes your book, but she likes another book also and can't decide which one she likes best. The one with the best and most complete market plan can easily be the means of pushing her in the direction of your book.

If you are planning on employing the services of a professional publicist, this should be listed in your market plan. Remember, this is at your expense so you must research the publicist very carefully.

A market plan is essential for an author and is an important item in your query package. (See an example in the Appendix.)

YOUR WRITER'S BIOGRAPHY

More commonly shortened to: writer's bio. The operative word here is: **writer**. The only information and credits that go into a writer's bio concern published material for which you have been paid. This may seem unfair, but it's the way we measure talent today.

This is *not* an autobiography. It includes *only* your writer's biography and your *platform*, if appropriate.

For example, including your platform would be necessary if you are writing about health and nutrition. You would include what experience or degrees you have to make you a credible person to be writing about the subject. If you are writing a novel that revolves around the CIA, your background as a former CIA agent, would be pertinent.

As in your query letter, if you wrote for the high school newsletter or were editor of your college paper, neither counts. List only writing which has been published and for which you received payment. There are exceptions such as editorial writing, especially if it's for the New York Times. Don't laugh, one of my friends got her start that way. We all need to start somewhere and an editorial in the Times is a tough nut to crack.

Above all, do *not* mention that you've been writing since kindergarten. Do *not* mention you have read all the mysteries you can find and you are sure yours is as good or better. In fact, at no time should you tell an agent how good your material is. He wants to make that judgment himself and telling him is only an irritant, which you don't need.

Along those lines, don't ever denigrate another author's writing. It's all right to say that your romance novels are similar to Nora Robert's, but never ever criticize her books or anyone else's to an agent or editor.

If you have written and published several books traditionally, you will list them in your writer's bio. Do not list self-published books. This bias may change in the future, but as of now, in only the most extreme circumstances, when sales figures are convincing, will an agent deal with self-published material.

I must insert here that many self-published books have not only subsequently been published traditionally, but have gone on to become best sellers: e.g. *Jonathan Livingston Seagull* and *A Celestine Prophecy* come immediately to mind. More recently, several self-published writers have become "discovered" by the major publishers and have been given excellent book deals.

The difference here is that *they have been "discovered"* by the publishers. They haven't submitted their self-published books to these publishers. They may have done so in manuscript form prior to being self-published, in fact, probably did and were turned down. Now—and this is the main point—only after they proved themselves by racking up fantastic sales on their own, did the big guys sit up and pay attention. So, the message is, don't submit your self-published book. Tally up sales in the six figures and they'll come to you.

Returning to your writer's bio, nonfiction books won't help to indicate how a fiction book will sell and vice versa. For the same reason, magazine articles or stories are not useful; however, if they are numerous, go ahead and list them or say something like: *36 articles published in national magazines.*

An exception would be—and there's always an exception, isn't there?—*stories published in literary magazines sometimes carry more weight with book publishers than those in general magazines.* An example would be Graywolf Press, a small but well-respected press, specializes in literary fiction and prefers writers to have published stories in literary magazines before submitting book manuscripts to them.

Suppose you've never published anything?

You are familiar with the old saw, you can't get a job without experience and you can't get experience without a job. *If you've published nothing,* as far as a writer's bio is concerned, you're in the same boat. But don't worry, that's the situation with most first time writers. So *what do you do about it?*

Nothing.

Whatever you do, do *not* try to try to construct a phony list of credits. Do *not* pull out those unpaid publications we put to rest earlier. Do *not* go back to "I've written all my life." If you have published any kind of story or article in a national publication, mention it in the body of your query letter and just skip a separate writer's bio.

I've spent a lot of time on this subject. The reason is that to an agent or editor, it's irritating to have a would-be client include this kind of irrelevant material in a query. It is yet another mark of the amateur. Is also one of the major concerns of the first time writer. You should remember that every writer was once a first time writer, and every agent was once a first time agent, so don't let your lack of a bio deter you from submitting a carefully prepared manuscript.

One last point:
Without a writer's bio, the agent will know you are unpublished, but it doesn't help your cause to push the

information at her; so don't volunteer this information with statements like: "This is my first novel." This is one place where her assumption is preferable to a stated fact, and definitely to a faked bio.

YOUR WORK AT LAST!

One of the most important pieces of material you will submit in this packet is a portion of your manuscript. Your query letter may be outstanding and your market plan may be excellent, but if your writing isn't also outstanding, you won't receive an offer for representation by an agent or an offer to publish your book by an editor.

Do not be in a hurry. Do not submit your manuscript until it is as good as you can make it. When you think that it's ready to send out, put it away instead.

What did she say?

Put it away instead. I know that's difficult to do. You're so anxious to get it out there after all these months, perhaps, years of work. Do it anyway. Put it away for a week. Take it out after a short break and read through it one more time. When you find that typo in the middle of your Chapter Three, you can hear me saying, "I told you so."

Leanne Burroughs, editor and publisher at Highland Press Publishing in Florida, says:

> *"The most important thing I share (with a hope-to-be-published-author) is to make your submission the best possible manuscript it can be. That means 'proof' it. If you have critique partners, use them. If you don't, read it through more than once before you submit it to a publisher. Use spell check. While it won't catch*

words that are spelled correctly that are actual words, it will catch many of your mistakes.

"No editor/publisher, wants to see manuscripts with spelling, punctuation, grammar mistakes. While the manuscript may be one of the best stories they've ever read, if the basic presentation of the manuscript reveals the story will require too much editing, most editors will tend to pass on it. They see too many manuscripts come in every day to have to spend hours on end editing to bring your story to the level it should have been when you first submitted it."

HOW MUCH OF MY MANUSCRIPT DO I SEND?

The obvious answer is the correct one: Submit exactly what the guidelines require, incorporating a dose of common sense.

For example, let's say the guidelines ask for the first three chapters or fifty-pages. Your third chapter ends on page 53. Send the full 53 pages. Suppose your chapter three ends on page 59. Find a good stopping point at or before page 50. Common sense.

Most important:
For fiction, always send the first chapter of the novel. If you are asked for the first three chapters, send them. If you are asked simply for three chapters, send the first three or if you have a chapter later in the book that you believe is especially good, send the first two chapters and that particular chapter. The agent wants to see the first chapter or the beginning pages. If possible, you want her to see the second chapter as well. Why? Read on.

If you are asked for ten, twelve or fifteen pages, send the first ten, twelve or fifteen pages. Don't pick a couple from here and a couple from there or all ten from a later chapter. The agent will suspect there is something wrong with your first chapters and that is not good.

If I seem to be belaboring this point, I am. It is extremely important. As I've said before, unpublished writers frequently use the first chapter for background material (back story). The story doesn't begin until chapter two which is why you should try and send chapter two if you can't get to the 'action' with a revision of the first chapter.

The agent needs to know if you have hooked the reader early on. That's why she wants the opening pages. It's to your advantage to send that chapter two, if possible.

A writer I knew casually, asked me to look at her manuscript some years ago. She had written an excellent mystery. The manuscript obviously had potential; however, the entire first chapter and well into the second was not only back story, it was absolutely unnecessary back story. I'll go further and say that it was downright boring. It killed her manuscript. I tried to gently tell her that, but I could see she wasn't buying it.

I suggested she send it to a 'book doctor' and gave her a couple of names. I saw her a year or so later at a book fair trying to sell her book. "How did it work out with the 'book doctor'," I asked. "Oh, it was terrible," she said. "She took so much out. I put it all back in and self-published it."

I don't know how much success she had selling the book, but I would be willing to bet she won't get many sales by word-of-mouth. It's too bad. Her basic story was good and her writing was good once she got past that awful beginning—the important part that determines whether or not the reader will continue. As we've seen time and time again, a professional can only give you the benefit of their knowledge and experience, but the author has to make the ultimate decisions. I just suggest you have an open mind

.

ADVICE FROM A PROFESSIONAL

Claudette Parmenter wears many hats. In addition to being a freelance writer, columnist and moderator of a writer's group, she is also an editor. I asked her to write a few words of advice for the readers of this book:

> *"Whether you are writing the query letter, book proposal or submitting a manuscript—Do Your Homework! A query letter is your sales pitch. Be honest, write clearly and don't rely on spell check from your computer. A query should take only one page or less. Keep it simple and to the point unless you're dealing with a textbook or other complicated project (and that would require a book proposal—see next chapter). Anything less than perfect will wind up in the 'round' file.*

> *"A manuscript must be scanned meticulously for grammatical errors and typos. It's very easy to forget a comma or quotation marks when you've been 'married' to your story for several months. Before you submit your manuscript to a publisher, put it in a drawer for a week or two then recheck the whole thing with fresh eyes. You'd be surprised at how many errors you will find on a project you thought was already perfect and worthy of submitting."*

Thank you, Claudette for echoing my sentiments Completely.

SUMMARY:

Write a tight query letter about the book—not about you. Write a one-page synopsis, including the conclusion. Develop a unique market plan. If you are new, you probably don't have a writer's bio, so skip that. Send as much of your manuscript as the agent's guidelines ask for (or use the information in Chapter Nine). Always include the first chapter/pages. Always be professional.

NEXT UP

Submitting fiction and non-fiction have many common elements, but there are important differences which we will explore in the next chapter on your journey to success.

CHAPTER TEN

HOW TO PREPARE A NON-FICTION PROPOSAL

As noted in Chapter Nine, at least 75 percent of the material I received was lacking in several areas. The same holds true for nonfiction proposals as for query packages for fiction manuscripts. A poorly prepared proposal can doom a good book idea before it ever has a chance at publication.

Your nonfiction proposal is composed of:

- A cover letter
- a cover sheet
- an overview
- a market section
- a list of comparison books
- promotion
- a mission statement (optional)
- an author's platform
- a list of what's necessary to complete the book
- a chapter-by-chapter synopsis
- sample chapters
- an appendix, if necessary

THE COVER LETTER

The cover letter for nonfiction, as opposed to a query letter for fiction, must accompany your proposal. A cover letter is shorter than a query letter. In this letter, you need only tell the agent that you are enclosing a proposal for *The Title of Your Book*. Additional material need only be included if there is something specific you want the agent to know up front, such as a *Name* of someone who has agreed to endorse the book, or even better, a foreword to be written by a well-known expert in the field in which you are writing.

FORMATTING THE COVER SHEET

The writing on the **_cover sheet_** begins about one-third of the way down on the page and may be slightly larger point than the twelve point font you will use throughout the proposal.

Under the title, in twelve-point font, centered, type "by" and, centered under that, your name. All of these will be separated by double spaces.

Double space down and move to flush left on the page. Type your contact information: name, address, e-mail address, land line telephone number, cell phone number and web site URL, if you have one. All this will be single spaced.
On the right-hand side of the page, opposite your name, type the word count if the book is complete, or the estimated completed word count, if it isn't.

Put nothing else on the cover sheet. No photos. No illustrations. No fancy fonts. (See sample in the Appendix.)

THE OVERVIEW

The overview, in addition to being a synopsis of what the book will be about, will include other useful information, such as your rationale for writing it. This is also where you will put the information regarding a person well-known in the field who has agreed to write an endorsement or a foreword, if such is the case. Such an endorsement/foreword can be an important selling point.

How the book is structured is included in this section. If it is divided into three parts, for instance, state this and comment on the how and the why you have made this decision.

The overview should conclude with the information that the book is or is not complete. If it is not, include an estimated date of completion. A general rule-of-thumb for this estimation is to decide how much time you think you will need and add three months to that.

Imperative: once you have made a commitment to a deadline for completion, keep it!

MARKETS FOR YOUR BOOKS

This section of the proposal gives you an opportunity to convince the agent there is a market for your book. Here, you will discuss all those groups of readers who can be expected to read your book. For example, if your book has to do with the Civil War, you can expect civil war buffs, of whom there are many, to buy the book. If you have a sub-theme, perhaps the use of horses during that era, you can add horse enthusiasts. Use your imagination here and you may be able to come up with several distinctly different groups of readers.

Note: The Markets for the Book section is not the same as a marketing plan, which is covered in the section titled Promotion.

THE COMPARISON BOOKS SECTION

In the **Comparison Books** section, you will list several—three at a minimum—books which are similar to yours. State the title of the book, its author(s), publishing house and year of publication. You may locate these books at on-line bookstores, libraries, or in physical bookstores. It is important for the publisher to see how your book is similar to others, but also unique.

Write a sentence or two about the focus of each book and write a sentence or two explaining how your book differs. In other words, if there are other books about Lincoln on the market and yours is also about Abe, why should a reader buy yours?

This can be handled in one of two ways. You may type your remarks about your book immediately after each comparison book, or you may list the comparison books with the focus of each and conclude by listing comments regarding your book and how it differs from the others.

Do *not* suggest that yours is "better." State some concrete differences in your approach. You might have approached the subject from his early years or his relationship with his wife, his children, his cabinet—any theme that differs from other books written about your subject.

THE PROMOTION

The promotion section of the proposal is often broken into smaller sections:

- author's mission statement
- the author's platform and his
- marketing plan.

Let's look at them separately.

THE MISSION STATEMENT

Essentially, a **mission statement** consists of a sentence or two outlining what you hope to accomplish by writing the book. You may or may not have a mission statement. If the topic of your book is a memoir, you may not; if it's related to a social problem, you will.

Your mission might be to empower women or the handicapped, or to bring a little known or understood disease to the awareness of the public.

Joan West

The mission statement of this book is my desire to empower unpublished writers by giving them the tools to understand and overcome the hurdles of publishing.

AUTHOR'S PLATFORM

The Promotion section includes the **Author's Platform**, which explains why you are the appropriate person to write this particular book. Credibility is another word for it. What is it about you and/or your career or life that will convince an agent, editor or ultimately the reader that you have the authority and expertise—the credibility—to write about your subject? From what *platform* do you speak?

An appropriate platform is essential for the author of a work of nonfiction. No publisher will consider a book about agriculture, for instance, written by someone raised in an urban environment, who has never been near the countryside, let alone a farm, and whose entire knowledge of agriculture has come from reading books about it. Granted, this is an extreme example.

The point is that you must be an expert on the subject you have chosen to write about in non-fiction.

That's not to say you can't become an expert, even in the case suggested above. You want to write about agriculture? Go ahead and read all you can about it and then go hire yourself out on a farm. Learn from first-hand experience about your subject, whatever it is.

CREDIBILITY

In non-fiction, credibility is of utmost importance. In their book, *The Complete Guide to Writing Fiction and Nonfiction and Getting it Published*, Pat Kubis and Bob Howland are clear about the consequences of inaccurate research. "In a nonfiction book, inaccuracy destroys your credibility as an authority figure." He reader must be convinced you have the background, and/or completed the research accurately or your book will be left lingering on the shelf.

NOTE: Even in a novel "other than science fiction and fantasy, inaccuracy will jolt the reader from the illusion of life you are trying to create, and, moreover, the reader will probably not believe your book."

For fiction, in addition to the credibility of your story, your platform is having already successfully published a novel or, better yet, novels. If you haven't any writing credits, see Chapter Nine, Author's Biography.

MARKETING PLAN

I discussed a **Market Plan** in the previous chapter. The particulars of a market plan for non-fiction are similar to those for fiction. The major difference is the type of audience to whom you will present your message. In fiction, you rely on establishing a brand, or name, potential readers will recognize. While this is true to some extend in non-fiction, you also have a 'built-in' audience for the subject matter. As we stated earlier, you can find groups and associations that may be a ready audience for your book. For example a book about a disease may be marketed to medical associations or support groups that are concerned with that illness. Helping a publisher see these markets is a very good way to convince him to invest in your book, but it is also a great way for you to determine if the book will have an audience prior to doing the essential research.

REQUIREMENTS

If your book is complete, you may not need this section, but if your manuscript is not complete, it is probably because additional resources are needed to complete the book and that is what this section is for.

Frequently, a work of nonfiction requires much research, often involving travel. When this is the case, finances may be a consideration. An author facing a large financial outlay may seek to have a commitment to publish before going forward. If this is the case, your requirements should be listed here so the publisher can decide if he wants to help with obtaining your 'valuable' book.

Even if finances do not present a problem, if the book is not complete because some research or interviews remain necessary, you will list these needs in this section.

You may have all the necessary resources, but you don't want to spend the months or years you believe the actual writing will take and you are hoping for a contract and an advance before committing your time to this ambitious project. You can mention your reluctance to spend the time, but I wouldn't say anything about the advance, if I were you. Much better to describe your need for financial backing to complete the necessary research.

Again, if the book is complete, you would omit this section.

CHAPTER SYNOPSIS

The publisher wants to see the structure of your book chapter-by-chapter in a non-fiction proposal. As noted in Chapter Two, a **Chapter-by-Chapter Synopsis** is usually a paragraph or two per chapter, the rule-of-thumb being a sentence for every page in the chapter. Remember, this is a flexible guideline. What is not flexible is that your writing must be concise and professional.

SAMPLE CHAPTERS

The requirement for **Sample Chapters** in a non-fiction proposal differs from the requirements in a fiction query. While it is important that the first chapter be sent along with a fiction query, this is not the case for nonfiction. If the first chapter is available, by all means include it; however, often in nonfiction, the first chapter deals with the content and structure of the remainder of the book, as it does in this book. When this is the case, the first chapter is the last one written, after the manuscript has been completed. In any event, include a couple of pertinent chapters, not to exceed fifty pages unless the publisher guidelines stipulate differently.

APPENDIX

You may or may not need an **Appendix** for your proposal, but most do. This is the section of the proposal where you will place a few samples of the types of items you anticipate including in the book, such as newspaper articles, photographs and various other documents. The purpose of these is to demonstrate your credibility.

PUTTING IT ALL TOGETHER

The non-fiction proposal format I've outlined is not absolute. Not every proposal will require all the sections discussed. Some will not need a mission statement or a resources needed section, or an appendix.

On the other hand, you may want to add a section which may benefit your particular book. For example, a section suggesting possible spin-offs would be an excellent addition if you contemplate a follow-up book.

THE SPIN-OFF

A **spin-off** is a book or books you plan to write which will be "spun-off" the current one. Let's take a look at that Lincoln book for example.

Perhaps you've written about his assassination? Therefore, you have had something to say about John Wilkes Booth. In researching John Wilkes Booth you learn he was not only an actor himself, but was the son of a famous actor father. He also had two siblings, a sister and an actor brother. Your spin-off might be about Wilkes' family. Agents and editors both love to know an author has follow-up books in mind. Think of it this way: marketing two or three books on a subject by a credentialed expert is far better than marketing just one.

FORMATTING YOUR PROPOSAL

When preparing your proposal, be sure to begin each section on a separate page. Center the title of the section at the top of the page. Don't drop down, as you will for the chapters of your book. Use double spacing throughout. Use an appropriate header as described earlier for your manuscript.

The exception—you knew there would be an exception, didn't you?—is in the Promotion section. Promotion will be your main heading followed by sub-heads for your Mission Statement, Author's Platform and Market Plan—all parts of your Promotion.

TABLE OF CONTENTS

When your proposal is complete, construct a Table of Contents which you will place between the cover sheet and the Overview. This is a Table of Contents for the Proposal, not for the book. Make sure your page numbers are in sequence and you are ready to submit your proposal.

Editor Claudette Parmenter enlarged upon her comments in the previous chapter regarding query letters for fiction by pointing out the advantage of a properly prepared book proposal: "A book proposal will show a targeted publisher or agent your ability to highlight and condense your proposed story and make the editor want to read more."

WHAT'S NEXT?

No author likes to face rejection letters, but in the next chapter, we will discuss this unfortunate, but essential aspect of transforming from a writer to an author. Do not be afraid. Read on.

CHAPTER ELEVEN

WHAT IF YOU RECEIVE A REJECTION LETTER?

One of the most difficult occurrences with which a writer must deal—if not the most difficult—is the receipt of a letter rejecting her manuscript or, more accurately, declining to represent the manuscript for publication. Even worse in this electronic age, is receiving an e-mail saying, "Thanks, but no thanks." That seems really cold and unfriendly, doesn't it?

Writing is not an easy task. It can be downright hard. Preparing a query package or a proposal for submission is time consuming and a pain in the neck to a writer who wants to be writing a book not a query letter or an overview. Nothing about the creation of a book from the writing itself to submitting it is easy, but nothing is more demoralizing than having this work you've labored over rejected.

The reality is that you are almost certain to receive rejections. Some writers put their finished manuscripts in the bottom of a drawer rather than submit them to an agent and open themselves up to rejection. This is a natural reaction. No one enjoys rejection, and a writer who doesn't develop a philosophy about rejection is in trouble. How you develop such a philosophy is personal, but develop it you must in order to keep writing.

DIFFERENT TYPES OF REJECTIONS
THE DREADED FORM LETTER

When the letter that arrives in your mail box is a printed form letter with no personal notation, you're disappointed. That's natural, but don't take it personally. Don't e-mail, write or telephone the agent to ask her why. Cross her name off the list and move on to the next name you have chosen.

118

THE PERSONAL NOTE

If you receive a personal letter of rejection, that's a plus. As I've said before—and will say again—agents are busy people. If one has taken the time to write to you, it is perfectly proper for you to write her a short note of thanks. Do *not* take this as an invitation to re-write the material and re-submit it unless she has specifically requested that you do so. Make a note beside her name. When you are ready to send out your *next* book, then you may send it to her with a note reminding her of the letter she had sent to you and thanking her once again. You might also say you hope you have successfully remedied whatever critique she had made before.

Author and editor, Claudette Parmenter offers this advice, "Don't take rejects personally or you'll have a hard time in this business. Writing is a business and must be viewed as such. If your story isn't accepted by an editor/publisher, send it to the next one on your list. Persevere and you will eventually succeed."

It might help to know some of the principle reasons agents reject material, so, read on and you may feel better.

REJECTIONS ATTRIBUTED TO THE AUTHOR

The manuscript needs additional work:
To say the manuscript is not as good as it should be does not necessarily mean the writing is not good. It frequently means simply that it needs more work. You have submitted it prematurely.

A common problem: The Rushed Ending:
There is a tendency, especially among unpublished writers to write "The End" too soon. Sometimes we're too close to our work and can't see this and other flaws the publisher may be responding to.

119

Remember that both Claudette Parmenter and I advised you to put what you consider the completed manuscript aside for a while and in a week or two revisit it? That's advice to take to heart. Use the time for R&R or, better yet, to write the outline for your next book. Stay busy.

Has anyone else read the book? Have you asked someone with a discerning eye, preferably someone who knows something about publishing—here is when being a member of a writing group is a help. If not, try to find such a person and ask him to read it and give you feedback. Hiring an editor at this point would be useful.

If you've done all you can, take the book out of its hiding place and read it once again and be sure it's as good as it can be.

Inappropriate submissions:
An obvious reason for the rejection of a good piece of writing is that you've sent the wrong genre to the wrong agent. Hopefully, I've mentioned this often enough that you won't do it.

Inappropriate word count:
Word count is often a cause for rejection. Judging from the queries I've received, many writers are unaware that some fairly standard rules apply in regard to works in the various genres. For example, a romance novel can have anywhere from 60,000 or 70,000 to 75,000 or 80,000 words, while mysteries have a little more leeway, say 60,000 to 90,000 words. These figures are approximate and not absolute, but as I've noted before, some publishing houses are extremely strict as to the word count of the various sub-genres within the parent genre so you really need to visit the specific website and examine the guidelines carefully.

Mainstream novels as a rule tend to run between 80,000 and 100,000 words, while thrillers and historical novels can be somewhat longer. Work from first time writers should almost never top 100,000 words regardless of genre.

Remember, these are estimates. Your major concern is not to write too long—over 100,000 words or too short—less than 50,000 words. You should also be aware that work between 20,000 and 50,000 words is considered a novella. Work over 50,000 words can be called a novel; although, 50,000 words would be a very short novel.

The word count for nonfiction is a bit looser than that for fiction. Memoirs should probably be somewhat under 100,000 words, other types may be longer; however, it's a good idea to abide by the caution to keep your work, the work of an as yet unpublished author, to 100,000 words or less.

Unbelievably, I once received a query from a writer who offered me a novel in excess of 500,000 words. He also mentioned that books two and three were in the works. This query shouted, "amateur." No writer who had done his homework would even consider submitting something of this length.

Suppose you have enough material to write a book of a couple of hundred or more pages. What do you do? You find a good stopping point and break it into two or even three separate books.

On the other hand, I've also received submissions of 11,000 and 15,000 words, which I've had to reject without even looking at them. Although, I must mention that these word counts would be fine for a children's or young adult book.

A one book author:
A manuscript might be rejected if the agent/publisher suspects it is a one-time deal. Agents don't want to acquire authors who have only one book in them. It takes a lot of effort and money to publish and promote an author. It isn't worth it to the agent or editor to work with someone when it's obvious that he can be expected to produce only one book.

Lack of a platform:
An author's lack of a platform (read: name recognition or recognized expertise in a specific field) ranks as a top reason for a manuscript to be rejected. In today's highly competitive publishing world, name recognition and/or occupying a unique position is becoming not only important, but necessary. If you don't have a platform at this time, see Chapter Ten for suggestions on how to begin to build a platform for yourself. It is that important.

Memoirs:
A memoir is almost guaranteed to produce enough rejection letters to paper that pesky bathroom wall so many unpublished writers talk about. The 'one-book author' rejection factors in here. It's one reason why it's so difficult for an ordinary person to get a memoir published.

Frank McCourt can write and get his bestselling *Angela's Ashes* published not only because it's a riveting tale but because he is a *writer with a known platform*. The publisher knows he will be writing books until the end of time. What is there about your memoir that makes it unique enough for a publisher to invest time, money and effort in a one-shot deal?

Some reasons for rejection which you cannot control

A saturated genre:

Even though you've done everything right, your manuscript may be rejected for a number of reasons that have nothing to do with your skill or the quality of your book.

For example, you have submitted a query for your romantic suspense novel to an agent who is known for handling romantic suspense, but she rejects it. It may be that at the time of your submission, she is overloaded with the genre. No matter how good your book may be, if the agent is currently "pitching" a similar work, she will not be able responsibly to accept yet another.

In addition, it may be that the entire industry is saturated and a specific genre has stalled out. If a specific genre is selling like wildfire, say thrillers, it might seem like a good idea to get on the bandwagon. But think about it. If just about everybody is writing and submitting thrillers, wouldn't you have a better chance for writing in a genre where the competition is not so great?

Also to be considered is the length of time it takes for a traditional publishing house to get a work published—from a year and a half to three years. By that time, the reading public may have moved on to another genre. You need to be ahead of the trend not catching up to the caboose.

Bottom line, don't try to be the next John Grisham or J. K. Rowling. Carve out a niche for yourself.

PERSONAL ISSUES FOR REJECTIONS
Agents are human:
The agent had a fight with her husband this morning or she may not like your first name.

This sounds silly, but we are all creatures of our biases and subject to our emotions. Most agents attempt to be objective, but you just might have the bad fortune to have your manuscript hit an agent's desk on a day when she is grappling with a personal problem which may cause her to judge your manuscript harshly. On the other hand, she might heartily dislike her Aunt Sarah and it's your bad luck that you named your protagonist Sarah.

What I'm trying to say here, is that all kinds of idiosyncrasies can play a part in our lives. If you begin to receive rejection letters, check out the possible reasons for them listed in this chapter. If you see a similarity, go back to the drawing board or in this case the computer and see what you can do to save your work. Or you could put it aside and begin to work on your next book, (or *continue* to work on it, because you should have begun your next book way before you had the chance to receive a rejection for this one).

THE FIRST BOOK JINX

Some say your first book never works, that you have to have one dud before you write the one that's a winner. It is hard to put aside that first masterpiece, but sometimes that is exactly what you need to do. The real author has more books inside him and should start working on his next one while he waits for agents and publishers to gobble up his first. And if that doesn't happen, set the first one aside and put what you have learned into the second and even better book.

LEARN FROM AND USE REJECTION

Above all, don't allow rejection letters to discourage you. Learn from them and keep submitting until you are fairly satisfied you have done your best. As we have seen there are many reasons, other than the marketability and quality of your book that could prevent a publisher/agent from taking it on, but that doesn't mean you can't change course and consider self-publishing. Many authors are increasingly looking at this option so if you are interested in self-publishing the next chapter is especially for you.

CHAPTER TWELVE

DO YOU WANT TO SELF-PUBLISH?

If you are considering self-publishing, the information in this chapter is designed to help you. You will also find several excellent books on the market that will lead you step-by-step through the maze of self-publishing (see the Appendix) options. You will find sufficient information between the covers of this book to get the job done, but I'm an advocate of reading, reading, reading.

TYPES OF SELF-PUBLISHING

Self-publishing houses come in many guises beginning with those to which you pay a bundle in exchange for doing it *all* for you from start to finish. Well, you have to write the book, of course, but that's all. You pay and they do it all...or so they say.

You may be more interested in those who will take over where your expertise leaves off and finish the job. You do as much as you can, then pay, and they do the rest...or so they say.

If you have still more expertise, you might look for one which allows you to serve as your own editor and designer. With this type, once you have a finished book in an electronic file, complete with cover, you simply upload it to their web site and in a very short time the Fed-X guy will be at your doorstep with a printed book with your name on the cover. These publishers vary widely in the services they offer. You do most of the work, then pay smaller amount, and they get your book made.

HOW MUCH CAN YOU DO YOURSELF?

The key factor in selecting a 'self-publishing' house is asking how much can you do yourself? The more you can do, or learn to do, the less you should have to spend for their services.

For most of us, the answer to that question is: Everything up to the printing and binding, depending on your expertise, or lack thereof, especially of the use of computer programs.

TEXT FORMATTING

If you know how to do the basics (such as, formatting to page size, margins and page breaks), there is no reason why you can't prepare the manuscript for printing. Most self-publishing houses make it fairly easy to accomplish this.

WHAT ABOUT THE COVER?

For cover preparation, your knowledge must be more sophisticated. You must know how to use a cover template, how to figure the size of the spine (The one I use is: number of pages divided by 2 X 0.0048 inches. Example: 320 page book: 320 divided by 2 = 160 X 0.0048 = a 0.768 inch spine), how to insert your author's photograph on the back cover, how to wrap the type around the photo and how to insert your cover art or photograph on the front cover. Many authors prefer to pay to have this work done for them, and since covers sell books that is not a bad idea if you have doubts of your abilities in this area.

CONVERSION OF FORMATS

For some book printers, the manuscript must be converted to PDF which can be done via a program called, Acrobat Professional. (My version is number 8. I believe some Microsoft programs can handle this also.) You need to read the specific instructions carefully since conversion must be done prior to uploading the manuscript on the printer's web site. For online e-publishers, such as Kindle, that is not required.

Most self-publishing houses will offer any or all of these services for a fee, or you can hire an independent contractor. Again it all depends on how much you can do yourself and your budget.

AN EXAMPLE OF DIY

To keep publishing costs low, I was able to learn many of the skills needed to prepare a book. For example, I am able to format the front and back covers, which includes deciding on an appropriate photograph or other art work, inserting it on the front cover and the author photo on the back cover; placing the title and any other necessary copy on the front; and formatting the material for the back cover to page size. This is a huge savings in prep costs.

By giving your cover technician the two completed pages to drop into the template, you reduce her time spent to less than an hour, which keeps your fee low.

I'M TERRIBLE WITH COMPUTERS?

Let me say a few words here about my abilities with computers so you don't feel so hopeless. Just beyond minimal, would be an appropriate description. When I began publishing, they were far short of minimal.

With the help of some people with expert knowledge, I have learned to do just about everything I need to do to prepare my books for publication myself. I still require help in some areas. I owe a great debt to those who have helped me in the past and those who continue to help me. However, my point is that electronics is neither in my field of expertise, nor do I find any particular pleasure in it; therefore, if I can do it, you can do it! And it will save you a lot of money.

LOOKING CLOSER AT MY SELF-PUBLISHING OPTIONS

As in any business, there are honest publishers and unfortunately scam artists who depend on an author's driving desire to have a book published to sell them a bill of goods. It is extremely important that you know what you are getting and this means you need to fully understand the terminology used in describing the many publishing options available to the self-publisher.

I asked Mary Lois Sanders to tell us in a few short paragraphs the differences between the types of self-publishers. By a welcome coincidence, she had just completed a paper about this very subject for the use of the 2012 Florida Writers Conference. Her definitions of vanity, fee-based and do-it-yourself publishers is very helpful.

VANITY PRESSES

You pay for a package of formatting, book cover design help, and a pre-determined number of books published. The house does little in the way of editing or even proofing—that's up to you.

FEE-BASED PUBLISHERS

You buy one of several publishing packages, which may include editing (from line editing to full book editing)—(for this type of editing, see book doctor in Chapter Seventeen or content editor in Chapter Seven) and the book production staff does everything from formatting to cover design to marketing plans. Many of these houses are quite large and may lock you into long-term contracts. Others are "boutique" style houses that work with you one-on-one to get your book published the way you want it. In either case the fees charged vary. The marketing from a fee-based house varies from basic (puts your book on Amazon and other online book sellers' websites) to advanced (runs your bookstore and actively markets through brochures and catalogues.)

DIY PUBLISHING

You do it all, or most of the work, (editing, proofing, formatting, cover design, etc.) and upload your PDF files to the website. These houses may also have a la carte services, e.g., formatting, cover design, editing. Once your book is published, you are charged a base price for the books you order. Some DIY's have web bookstores. Most will set you up on Amazon.com and other distributors and you earn royalties based on online sales. Most of your earnings will depend on your own marketing activities.

FULL SERVICE PUBLISHING

To add to what Mary Lois has said about vanity presses, I also call them, full service fee-based publishing houses, that is those publishing houses from whom you buy the complete package, which includes X-number of copies of the printed book. You simply mail a typed manuscript or send an electronic file of the unformatted manuscript and a hefty check and, in a reasonable length of time, they send you a box of books.

LOCAL PRINT SHOPS

Local print shops are an alternative to these options and can be just what a writer is looking for, depending on what services you need and how much you are willing to pay for them. Some local printers can do the same type job as the full service publishers discussed above or they can provide you with just printing the finished, formatted manuscript, if you have the know-how to prepare it.

For printing only, the price will depend on the number of copies you order at one time. The more you order, the lower the per-book price will be. Most local printers require a run of at least one hundred copies. Fewer copies would not be worth the cost of setting up their printers.

My partner, and I chose this method for our small press publishing business, prior to the advent of electronic publishing, and we were pleased with the result. We found many advantages with this method. We got to know the printer and the staff and they got to know us. This allowed us the ability to communicate clearly with one another. Electronics can't replace face-to-face contact.

Convenience is another positive factor for dealing with a local printer. We could stop in and speak with the printer about any concern that occurred. We were able to pick up the finished books or he would deliver them to us for a nominal charge. He would also ship our books directly to a client when we needed that service.

Sadly, the difference in price, due to the fact that from a POD publisher (see the next section of this chapter), we are able to have one or two printed at a time as opposed to the three to five thousand necessary to obtain a reasonable price from the local print shop, can be decisive.

CO-OP PUBLISHING

One other type of publisher fits into this category: the co-op publisher. These houses split the cost of publishing between the author and themselves in a proportion agreed upon between them. I'm sure they also negotiate who does what in regard to preparing the manuscript and cover for printing.

PRINT ON DEMAND (POD)

Since traditional publishing has become so difficult and because there are so many writers who want to have their work published, a new breed of publishing house has arisen in the industry. These publishers are called POD, because that is exactly what they do: they publish your book only when you "demand" it and only in the number you "demand."

Translated, that means they will publish as many books at one time as the author is willing to purchase, from a single copy to hundreds or thousands. They will format, create your cover, supply an ISBN, each for a price, of course; or you can upload a completed book in an electronic file, including cover, and they will do the printing only.

This type of publishing is hurtful to traditional methods of self-publishing, but a boon to writers. As noted, if a writer wishes, he can now upload his formatted manuscript and cover to a web site. He can order a print proof or not, as he desires, or he can download a proof as soon as his material has been approved and when satisfied that all is correct, can order as many or as few copies—even only one—as he needs.

In other words, you the writer, have the option of having them do all the work—for a price—or you can do it, upload it and, Voila!, out comes a book.

For writers, the appearance of print-on-demand can be likened to the invention of the proverbial sliced bread. On average, they make your job quicker, easier and less expensive.

Lois and I chose Create Space—an arm of Amazon.com.—a choice which has made our job infinitely easier and more cost effective. There are other companies who may be every bit as good. We just happened to choose this one and our experience has been positive.

ELECTRONIC PUBLISHING

E-books are a result of electronic publishing. These books are not printed on paper. They exist only as electronic files which can be purchased by owners of electronic readers. Two of the major electronic publishing venues at this time are Kindle, a unit of Amazon.com and Nook, a unit of Barnes & Noble Booksellers. There are others. A few minutes on Google will probably give you an additional list of electronic publishing sites.

In this book, I am concerned with electronic publishing as it pertains to the *writer*. I'll leave it to others to describe the pros and cons for the reader.

For writers, author Olive Church considers e-publishing a boon where expense is concerned. "The least expensive path to taking the self-publishing route may be the new e-publishers," she says, "because neither they nor you will be dealing with paper and postage. Everything is on-line, including the cover."

In order to post your e-book, you must first format the manuscript and design the cover. These will differ from the manuscript and cover used for a print copy of the book. In a print copy, you have a certain number of blank pages. You will want to eliminate those for your e-book. You also will not need to design a spine or a back cover. Neither are seen in the on-line version of the book.

Uploading the formatted manuscript is a simple maneuver, as is assigning a price to the book. Each site has its own set of rules and requirements. Decide which site you want your book to appear on. At this time, you may post your book on any or all of them at once. Check them out to be sure. With certain specific exceptions—there's that word again—when utilizing special offers at the various sites.

Once you have made your choice or choices, familiarize yourself with each site's individual set of instructions and proceed. After the book is posted, you may go back in and make changes at any time.

You will receive a certain percentage of the price for each book sold. At this time, books priced above $9.99 on Amazon.com pay roughly 35 percent of the price of the book, 70 percent for books priced at $9.99 and below. Special set-ups are provided for books priced below $2.99. Some sites, Amazon.com for example, offer your books to several other countries at a lesser royalty. Check all of this out when you are ready to upload your material. Things change rapidly in this industry.

TRADITIONAL BOOKSELLERS ON-LINE

While you may not succeed in placing your book on the shelves of one of the large chain bookstores, you have an excellent chance of having them listed with their online websites. Unless you have been living in Outer Mongolia for the past few years, you know to list your book with amazon.com, but don't forget others.

Barnes & Noble maintains a Small Press Department in New York City. Go to their home page at barnesandnoble.com. In the middle of the bottom area of the page, you will find: Publisher & Author Guidelines. Click on that. The Guidelines contain all the information you will need to submit your title for sale on their website.

ADVICE FROM AN INDUSTRY VETERAN

In today's harsh publishing climate, many authors trade the time, effort and headaches involved in attempting to publish traditionally for the time, effort and headaches involved in self-publishing right from the start.

Consider author and publisher Mark Newhouse. Mark believes, "...in the traditional model as verification that your book is meeting the required standards" and often publishes via the traditional route. His publication list is impressive having had stories published in various periodicals such as Newsday, Cricket and Cobblestone Press and having been published by traditional publishers such as Educational Activities and Quixote Press to name only a few.

Yet Mark often turns to self-publishing under his own house label, Earth Kids Publishing, and now AimHiPress, with partner, Linda terBurg, and using Create Space for much of his printing. Why? "Because of the time saving. After your book is accepted," he says, "there is still a wait for as long as four years to publication at some traditional publishing houses."

Mark is extremely knowledgeable of the publication industry and is generous with his time and energy in helping writers in whatever area he can. He is responsible for creating The Writers' League of The Villages, an organization which grew in a year from about 40 to 165 members, who organize and participate in a yearly Authors' Show-case and numerous other activities of benefit to writers.

When I interviewed him recently for this book, he cautioned me to be sure to warn writers to guard against scams in the self-publishing field. Mark suggests that writers check out the web sites of Writer's Beware and Editors Predators.

Mark also cautioned about those seemingly reputable agents/publishers who charge a considerable amount of money up front. One for example offers a choice of two contracts to the writer. In one contract, the writer pays $1,000 and his book will be published immediately or he can pay $200 plus sell 100 pre-publication orders. In this second contract, only after he has paid the $200 and taken the 100 orders, presumably pre-paid, will a book be published. His advice: "Read the contract very carefully even if you need a microscope for the fine print."

However you have arrived at the decision, if self-publication is your choice, go for it and good luck. But add careful research since good luck comes with good old hard work.

WHAT'S NEXT?

Whether you publish traditionally or self-publish, today's highly competitive climate demands you develop ways to market your book/s. In the next chapter we will explore the aspect of being an author many writers dislike. Any idea what that may be?

CHAPTER THIRTEEN

HOW DO YOU PLAN TO SELL YOUR BOOKS?

Marketing is a dirty word to most writers. That attitude is not without merit. Writers are writers. They're not sales people.

Think about it, can you think of a profession that demands more solitude than writing? Most writers are at heart introverts. Yes, some writers collaborate and some, like Hemingway and his cohorts, are able to focus on their writing oblivious to what's going on around them. They can write while sitting at a tiny table on a sidewalk in front of a café on the left bank of Paris, but even they operate within a bubble of solitude they have drawn around themselves.

"I wrote the book. It isn't fair to ask me to sell it," I've heard writers say and I agree. I feel the same way about my own writing. A pox on those who demand that we do it, but do it we must, because no one else is going to.

"If my book is published by one of the major publishing houses," a writer may ask, "won't they take care of all of that?" The answer with some few exceptions is, "No."

If you are a president or former president or Nora Roberts or John Grisham, then, yes, the publisher will spend his budget dollars on you. If you are one of their mid-list writers, a small budget usually will be allotted to your book, but you still have to do most of the grunt work yourself. Even the big guns have to move out of their comfort zones to travel around the country appearing on just about every late night television talk show, plus a few of the daytime and early morning shows thrown in.

Of course, we'd all like to lose a little sleep in order to appear on all those shows in exchange for the monumental publicity they generate, but it's not likely.

If you are published by a small press, sometimes called a boutique press, or if you are self-published, the entire burden of getting it out there is going to fall on you. As successful author and marketer Mark Newhouse says, "Therefore, unless you plan to be a marketer, it doesn't pay to publish a book if your main objective is to have it sold."

It's a fact of publishing life, so get used to it, stop fighting it and get out there and sell your book.

I don't like marketing. I don't know how to market.

Don't feel too badly; you're not alone. This chapter and the three chapters that follow are designed to give you a leg up on this important but onerous task. I'll begin in this chapter with one of the types of marketing that you'll become involved in: traditional marketing. I can also refer you to our two great companion books: How to Sell Your Books Workbook by Linda terBurg, and How to Sell Your Books Checklist by Mark H. Newhouse. The three of us have the same goal: to help you "tame the marketing monster".

TRADITIONAL MARKETING

ADVERTISING

Along with placing your book in bookstores, advertising in newspapers and magazines and on radio and television are considered to be traditional marketing.

Buying space in newspapers or magazines or buying time on radio or television is expensive. The budgets of most independent writers won't stretch to include any of these sources. Placing your book with a bookseller is not automatic.

You must first be accepted as a vendor by a nationwide distributor. This, however, is far from a routine chore. So what's a 'poor' writer to do?

PAID NEWSPAPER ADS

If you are willing, and able to afford this type of advertising, you should consider hiring someone who is experienced in the field to create your ad. A well designed ad with a good visual of your book can generate a lot of interest. On the other hand, an amateurish design will garner no attention or a negative response. Your job of marketing is difficult enough without an expensive, poorly designed ad working against you.

FREE PUBLICITY

If you are not able to afford putting an ad in the newspaper, try getting some **free publicity** locally.

Contact the appropriate editor or reporter at your local newspaper. Tell her about the book you have published and ask if the paper would like to have someone interview you. If you are too shy or modest to do this, ask a friend to call for you. Most newspapers, especially local ones, are glad to do it. A newspaper editor has a lot of space to fill every day.

Once you have made an appointment for the reporter to come to your home, decide ahead of time the best spot to have your photo taken—holding up your book, of course. Consider what you are going to wear. Be sure it's something that will photograph well and not distract from the book. Be prepared, but also be prepared for the professional photographer to design what they think will be an effective shot.

Talking to a reporter requires preparation. Know what you are going to say. Imagine what questions the reporter might ask you.

If such interviews are a regular feature of your paper, read a few of them to get an idea of where the reporter will be going in the interview. Write down on a piece of paper a few details that you don't want to forget. Keep it inconspicuous, but near.

Mention the title of the book as often as possible without being pushy. If you have been traditionally published, mention the publisher. If you're self-published, skip that.
Mention how the book can be obtained. If you have upcoming events—a launch party, a book signing, etc.—mention them.

On a separate piece of paper, type your name, the title of the book, the publisher's name (if pertinent), where and how the book can be obtained and a list of upcoming events. Give this to the reporter before she leaves. Even though she has made her own notes, your neatly typed sheet will serve as a reminder to her.

RADIO & TELEVISION
The cost of national radio or television advertising would be prohibitive for any but a writer of independent means, one who is willing to make the investment. For most writers, local stations or channels offer more reasonable rates, which ordinarily depends on the locale and the distance the station covers. Check the numbers in the telephone book or your computer search engine, (e.g. Google), and give your local broadcasters a call. You have nothing to lose and much to gain.

If you find the rates, even for radio are too steep. You can find freebees and low-cost venues from your local newspaper. The operative word is local. Start your campaign locally. The fact is unless you already have a large platform, you would not stand much of a chance of having *The Washington Post*, *The Chicago Tribune* or *The New York Times*, sending a reporter to interview you and take your photo for an article in their papers, but local papers may jump at the chance. Similarly you might not have a prayer of having ABC, NBC or CBS invite you to be a guest on one of their broadcasts; however, your local station might welcome a story about a local writer and her accomplishments.

STEPS TO LOCAL BROADCASTING

1. Obtain a list of radio and television stations within driving distance of your home.
2. Listen/watch the programs. Identify programs on which you would be a good fit.
3. Separate the stations and channels into lists of competing markets.
4. Make another list from only one of your market lists. Do not approach stations from competing markets at the same time.
5. Prioritize this list.
6. Send your press kit. (See Chapter 16)

After you've done your homework to select your target broadcaster, it's time to court them. Instead of flowers and candy, send off a press kit. Begin at the top of your list with only a few stations. Send each a press kit (see Chapter Sixteen).

FOLLOWING UP A PRESS KIT

In their *Getting Published* issue of that great series, *The Complete Idiot's Guide*, the editors Sheree Bykofsky and Jennifer Basye Sander suggest that you wait a week after sending the kit, then call and ask for the producer of the particular show you have chosen. "Tell him you are following up on a press kit you sent." Ask if he received it and ask if he has any questions.

If he says he has received it, especially if it has interested him enough to have questions about it, you're ahead of the game. Now is the time to begin what *Getting Published* calls "your 30-second phone pitch.

30 Seconds? Are you kidding?
"Why 30-seconds?"

"The producer won't give you much time, so try to hook him quickly," Bykofsky and Sander urge.

If the producer says he doesn't know anything about it, you'll have to launch immediately into the phone pitch so one excellent piece of advice from *Getting Published* is to practice it beforehand. As noted, 30-seconds is not much time, so you need to be ready to go with it and confident in what you are going to say.

Don't let this time limitation frighten you. Try it. You'll be amazed at how much you can squeeze into those few seconds. But it's vitally important that you have what you are going to say firmly in your mind.

I remember a time in the beginning of my career as a literary agent. I called a publisher in New York expecting a secretary or receptionist to answer the call. Imagine my surprise when the owner of the company himself answered. I gulped and gave him my pitch for a specific book. "No," he said, "that's not for us." "Well, as long as I have you on the line," I stammered, "may I tell you about a couple of other books?" "Go ahead." I blurted out a few facts about two other books I represented. "Nope, not for us," he said, "but call me if you get anything else."

Now, maybe I would have struck out even if I had been better prepared, but I've always had the nagging feeling that the first book really was for him and had I my pitch firmly in mind, and rehearsed, and not been startled by the man himself answering the phone, he would have at least looked at the book. Don't let that happen to you.

Before you pick up a phone, *know* what you are going to say and have some backup to counter with in case the person on the other end doesn't respond as you expect him to.

By the way, if the producer is unavailable, or will not talk to you, ask to speak to the program director. She is in charge of all the shows on the schedule and a great secondary contact.

Be positive. Remember, as with local papers, local radio stations and television channels have lots of air time to fill and most are delighted to spotlight a local celebrity.

When you do get lucky, be sure to be professional. This means your appearance as much as anything else. You may well be able to complete your radio interview via telephone from your own living room where no one will see you. Television is a different matter. Be sure you are dressed as a professional author and that your vocabulary is professional. One exception: the television host may be happy to have something off-beat to liven up the interview. It's here that my would-be client's alligator might come in handy—if it pertained to your book's theme, that is. Just be sure whatever you do isn't too quirky and that it remains in good taste.

A caution: As small press publishers, one of our first authors was invited to speak on her local radio station. She was excited, as were we. When we listened to the transcript of the show, we were appalled to hear she had failed to mention the title of her book or how a potential reader could purchase it.

Another of our authors, also while being interviewed on a radio show, mentioned the title of the book we had just published for her only once. She spent the remainder of the interview talking about a previous book she had published which is now out of print.

Make notes. Remind yourself to *talk about the book...tell where the book can be purchased.* Don't miss your big chance.

PLACING YOUR BOOK IN BOOKSTORES

Book stores come in two categories: the major chain stores and the independents. Usually, the independents obtain their stock from two sources: book distributors and individual writers. The chains with some few exceptions, buy only from the distributors. What this means to the self-published author is that he is essentially left out where selling to the chains is concerned.

When having your printing done by Create Space, for example, for a small payment ($25 at this time) they will take care of extended distribution for you. The difficulty here is that companies like Create Space, understandably, will not accept returns; therefore, chains like Barnes & Noble will not deal with them. So, your book is still not in the chains.

I've looked in every corner and under the rug and the only option I've come up with is for the individual self-published writer to visit the chain booksellers in his area, show his book to the manager and guarantee to accept returns and, perhaps, she will stock one or two of his books.

The bottom line is: marketing self-published books in traditional marketing avenues is extremely difficult. But, don't despair. You're a writer. You're smart. Read the next couple of chapters. Draw up a plan, taking advantage of every non-traditional marketing idea you can come up with. Others have done it successfully, so can you.

CHAPTER FOURTEEN

HOW ELSE DO YOU PLAN TO SELL YOUR BOOKS?

After you've obtained as many venues as you can for the sale of your book through the traditional means—newspapers, radio, television and bookstores—discussed in the previous chapter, it's time to move outside the box. This chapter lists a few ideas. Be inventive. You will find a host of other outlets for sales.

RETAIL AND SERVICE STORES

Many venues for placing your book for sale are available to you other than the obvious ones such as book stores. It's up to you to get out and find them.

Try any independent store within traveling distance, not just independent bookstores, but also independent grocery stores, drugstores, gift shops, photo shops, mailing stores, beauty salons, even dress shops. The list is endless.

A writer of my acquaintance, places her books in the beauty salon where she has her hair done.

One of my writers, Olivia Claire High, not only places her books (The Crystal Angel, Rose Cottage, Dreams: Shadows of the Night), at the Curves in her town of Oroville, California, where she practices her exercises, but the proprietor allows her to have signings there whenever she debuts a new book. Claire is extremely grateful to her, and the publicity from newspaper notices of the signings are great PR for the exercise business.

PREPARING FOR SALES

If you are going to look at the various shops around you as possible markets for your book, you need to make a few preparations.

Display Racks:

Purchase some sort of display racks. These don't have to be expensive—just something attractive in which to display your books. On the internet, you'll find listings of companies where you can order what you need online. If you can, get the type of display with a slot for a sign.

Display Signs:

Have signs of an appropriate size made. Do you have a Staples near you? They do a good job of this. I'm sure other office supply stores do also, as do local print shops.

Business Cards/samples:

Introduce yourself as a resident of the area and present the person to whom you are speaking with your card. You do have cards, don't you? If you have had bookmarks made (see Chapter Sixteen), you might sweeten the pot by offering to supply one for each book sold.

Commissions:

Be sure you know what percentage of the retail price you are prepared to offer the proprietor of the shop before you approach her. Don't trust to chance. Having a fuzzy idea in your head about how you are going to approach the person in charge won't get you anywhere. Construct a detailed outline or a list of concrete steps you must take and follow it.

BOOK PARTIES

Book launches and parties are fun and a great way to introduce your books to neighbors and friends.

Contact some of your neighbors and friends. Ask if they would like to have a "Book Party." They invite their friends and neighbors and supply refreshments and you bring a stack of your books.

Be prepared to offer one as a door prize and give one to the hostess for her efforts. Also give your hostess a percentage of the sales of the book. This will serve as an incentive to have the party in the first place. To guarantee the greatest number of sales, offer her a greater percent or another gift if sales go above a certain dollar amount that you set. Suggest to her that she use her copy to obtain sales from friends who are unable to attend the party.

Don't forget to make a pitch for how nice a gift the book would make. This can encourage multiple sales.

Be sure to have some paper and pencil games prepared or athletic ones depending on the crowd. Have small, inexpensive trinkets as prizes. In fact, if you have access to a wholesale market or have happened on a good sale, you could buy a door prize, rather than giving a book. Make the event fun and others may want to host book parties for you too.

FUNDRAISERS

Perhaps a local charity would like to sell your book. Offer the book to them at a discount and everyone wins. You could offer a large discount for going over a specific number of sales.

Local animal shelters usually don't have access to many fundraisers. They would make good partners for you, especially if your book features an animal.

Along this line, sometimes a company will buy a supply of books to give to their customers if the topic of the book is appropriate for their product.

BOOK SIGNINGS

Ask your local independent bookstore or even your local exercise business or beauty salon if they will allow you to have a book signing on their premises. They benefit by receiving a percentage of the retail sales and by the publicity you will generate to get people to attend.

You can try the big chains and you may have success, but our experience is that they want only well-known writers for their signing events. One of the big chains in my area installed a shelf for local writers. Check yours out. If they don't have one, suggest it.

If a large bookseller does agree to host a signing for you, they will probably put an ad in the local paper in addition to in-store posters ahead of time. Be sure you also contact the newspaper, even if you have already been interviewed by them. They will probably either give you another interview or at least post a notice in their coming events section. Don't forget to post a notice on as many online venues as you can think of (more about this later in the chapter).

During the book signing, don't sit passively behind the desk. Walk around and talk to the customers, but don't treat them as customers, but as friends who will benefit from reading your book.

When I was a literary agent, one of my clients who had written a western novel, dressed up in western garb. He is a tall man and looked very imposing as a western hero.

Even more daring, another client, Olive Church, dons an enormous pink feather boa with a pink dress to match to attend her book signings as her character, Izzy Auld. Olive described it this way: "Scattered around my table were small piles of Hershey kisses candy. I'd palm some and as I walked around would hold out my hand to passers-by. I'd provocatively ask, 'How about a kiss?' Pause. 'Chocolate, that is.' They invariably laughed, took the candy and took a second look at my book." Olive said she not only uses this gimmick at book signings, but at book fairs and conferences as well.

Of course, you can't leave your table without someone tending it. If the bookstore doesn't provide an employee—and chances are they won't—bring a friend with you.

Another idea for a book signing is a group signing. Gather a group of writers to appear together, if you can arrange to have a specific theme, such as inspirational books or romantic novels, so much the better.

BOOK DISTRIBUTORS

Chances are you will only get your book into the data bases of the chains by being accepted by one of the major distributors (Ingram, Baker & Taylor, for example). As noted earlier, becoming a vendor for one of these distributors is extremely difficult and if you do manage to jump that particular hurdle, your book probably wouldn't be put on a store shelf if it is self-published. Bookstore space is very limited and tends to be for popular authors and large publishers.

The advantage to you is that once you are in the data base of a chain, anyone can order the book from the customer service desk in the store even if it is not on their shelf. It's up to you to get the word out about your book's availability.

The down side of listing your book with one of the major distributors is dealing with the returns. Most bookstores will accept your book only if you guarantee that unsold books may be returned to you. This can be a real stickler.

Both Lois and I work with one of the major distributors. They return books by one of the private shipping companies, as opposed to the United States Post Office.

Why does this matter?

Because the shipping companies charge much more than the Media Mail service offered by the Post Office. Just recently, a book was returned to me which sold for $13.95. If the book had sold, the distributor would have sent me a check for $6.28. I paid an additional $7.43 for the return shipping. Do the arithmetic: So far, this "sale" has cost me $7.43 + $2.47 my original shopping cost. And books can be returned for any reason.

Not only is it costly, but often the returned books are packed in such a haphazard manner they are no longer saleable. (This may not happen with all distribution companies, so I am not telling you not to try them. I just present the facts as they have happened to me. Be forewarned and be careful is much better than signing and being surprised.

CATALOG SALES

Catalog sales are big business. We receive several catalogs a month listing books of all types and at all prices. Thousands of catalogs exist selling all types of products. In fact, so many catalogs exist that directories are printed to list the catalogs! Tom and Marilyn Ross list six of the major ones in their "must have for authors thinking of self-publishing" book, *The Complete Guide to Self-Publishing.*

The cost of most of these directories is more than the average writer wants to pay, but the Ross' say *The Catalog of Catalogs* is affordable and their favorite. For others, try your local library or search engine.

After you have perused a directory and selected one or two that might carry your book, Tom and Marilyn Ross suggest, "Call and request a copy," then, "Study it. Consume it. Think about it."

At this point, they advise you to call again and ask for contact information about the buyer and "Request any available submission forms or guidelines."

Because getting your book into a catalog is so difficult, *The Complete Guide to Self-Publishing* goes into great detail. In fact, it devotes four-and-a -half pages to the subject including a Catalog Information Sheet example for you to follow in developing one for your book.

It's a lot of work and time consuming, but if you are successful, the return to you in sales could be phenomenal.

LIBRARIES

Not all libraries are alike. Some will let you come and talk about your book and will allow you to bring copies of the book for sale. Some will let you talk about the book, but won't allow sales. Others will allow you to do a workshop. The work-shop can either be about writing, how and why you wrote the book, and your experience publishing it, or if the book is nonfiction, your workshop can be on the topic of the book.

For example, a library located a couple of towns away asked me to do a workshop based on my previous book, *An Agent Speaks*. I will now be able to expand it to include publishing as well as material from an agent's point of view. This additional topic will encourage greater participation in the workshop. It adds interest for me as well as for those attending.

The librarian kindly gave me permission to sell books and has arranged for me to do an interview on a local television show to promote the workshop along with Lois who will appear on the same show to promote her appearance with a group of writers of inspirational books. (Her book, *Essays on Living with Alzheimer's Disease: The First Twelve Months,* certainly fits in that category.)

You might also use the idea noted under the **_Book signing_** heading, earlier in this chapter, and suggest to the librarian that you and she can put together a group of writers for an Authors' Showcase.

Even if the library you approach—and don't forget to branch out to libraries within your driving range—won't allow you to sell your books, go anyway. It's good publicity and you will be allowed to tell those who attend where they can obtain the book. Be sure to distribute cards with this information on them. Ask the librarian if you may put a batch of cards and/or bookmarks on the checkout desk. No opportunity is too small. Don't miss a one.

PRESENTATIONS/WORKSHOPS

Presentations and workshops are excellent vehicles for getting your book known and for sales. If you can manage to arrange for one presentation or workshop every week, you'll be well on your way to getting your name and the title of your book established.

This may not be as difficult as you might at first think. Club program chairmen, like newspaper editors and radio and television program directors, need to fill their calendars with interesting and entertaining programs for their members. How do you find them? Watch your local paper daily for news of local clubs. You can almost always find a name somewhere in the notice or article and there's your contact person.

While they might not be interested in hearing you talk about your book—that would have the earmark of a book signing— they might be interested in your road to becoming a published author. You know yourself, your book and your local community better than anyone, think up a good hook and go out there and start signing groups up.

If you are a shy author, perhaps you have a friend or relative who would be willing to act as "agent" for you. Just remember your book has a real benefit for your reader, as does your presentation. They will want you.

Not all books lend themselves to workshops, but if yours does this is the perfect venue for talking it up and selling some copies.

If not a workshop, how about a series of classes? How about your local adult learning center?

Most high schools and colleges, especially two-year institutions offer a wide variety of educational opportunities. Offer to give your one-time workshop or series of classes. You may even receive a small check for your services and normally all of your students will buy a copy of your book, which will be your textbook.

I have enjoyed making presentations and conducting workshops all over my state. I've talked to college groups, writing groups, groups at libraries, church groups—whatever group will sit still and listen to me. In addition for several years, I taught publication classes in our community's Lifelong Learning College. It gave me the chance to keep the skills I learned as a college professor from rusting and, since teaching is close to my heart, it gave me the opportunity to continue in a modified way after retirement from the classroom. Once again, use your imagination and you'll find many opportunities.

BOOK/CRAFT FAIRS

Most communities sponsor book fairs at some time of the year. On the one hand, they present a great way to promote your book to hundreds of people at one time. If it's a large enough fair, and if the topic of your book has universal appeal, you can do very well.

On the other hand, the competition is steep at a book fair. Look how many other authors surround you, all with books to promote. Your book has to have appeal or you risk not earning your table fee back.

Having said that, you might think a fair which is not specific to books might be a better bet. Not necessarily.

For three years, I attended a Vendor's Fair and never did earn the table fee back. Why?

One reason was that people didn't come to the fair to buy books. All sorts of vendors offered their wares from beautiful hand-quilted handbags to wood carvings to beauty products to Christmas ornaments. Craft fairs may not be the best venue for selling books. (The only one of my books that ever sold at that fair was *CATS: Short Stories about Cats* and I had to reduce the price to rock bottom in order to even sell that one.)

Another reason why I didn't do well at that particular fair was that just inside the front door stood long tables filled with paper and hard cover books for fifty cents apiece. What chance did my books have?! Before you enter a fair, check it out. Ask questions of previous vendors. Be cautious before you spend your money.

In a fair of this type, the content of your book will make a great difference in determining your sales. The only other writer at this fair was selling her cookbooks. Although the industry reports a slight downturn in their sales recently, cookbooks are universally popular. This same author writes historical novels, but has written a few cookbooks on a historical theme for just such an occasion. Clever!

NON-LOCAL BOOK FAIRS

Some book fairs in states other than your own, may allow authors to participate by sending copies of their books to be displayed at their fairs. Some of these require a fee—sometimes quite stiff—and others will offer the service free.

A couple that I am aware of are: the Maryland Book Fair and the Virginia Book Fair (see Appendix). Let me say that I have entered a few of these fairs paying a fee with no sales resulting. This year, I plan to enter a couple which require no fee. (I cannot actually recommend them because I have not yet participated in them. I offer the information for your consideration as possible venues.)

No matter from which angle you approach it, selling your book is challenging and requires you to be resourceful. For example, one of my writers successfully went door to door with his book; however, I wouldn't advise that. But I do advise you to use your imagination and you will come up with many unique nontraditional ways to sell your book.

BOOK REVIEWS

I've left the question of reviews until last, because I'm ambivalent about them for unpublished authors. First of all a review from a known reviewer is extremely difficult for an unpublished author to acquire. But that shouldn't stop you from looking locally.

Local book reviewer Terri Schlichenmeyer (bookwormsez@gmail.com) told me the best way for a writer to submit a book for her review. She said that if she is assured a book is available nationally, to just send it to her. To be 'nationally available' is a legitimate requirement. After all if she reviews a book favorably and her readers go to a national chain and are told they don't carry the book, they will become unhappy with the reviewer and the reviewer loses credibility.

Kirkus Reviews is an example of a professional reviewing service. What makes it interesting is they have added a 'pay-for-review' option. Previously they only reviewed non-self-published books, but the new program includes these. So is it worth paying for this type of review? A few people have recommended having Kirkus review your book since a review from a professional is difficult to get and adds some legitimacy. Others have not been enthusiastic, mentioning the fee and the possibility that if it's a bad review, you're stuck with it!

I have some concerns about paying for reviews, and certainly no author wants a negative review, but I'm not sure this fear is an appropriate attitude. It's something you'll have to decide. The bottom line is that a good review, if you can get one, is a great tool for promoting your book.

WHAT'S NEXT?

Perhaps the greatest change in book publishing is on-line marketing. For many authors, it is becoming the focus of their selling strategies, but first they have to navigate the maze of on-line options. Let's see if we can help.

CHAPTER FIFTEEN

ONLINE MARKETING

This is a fairly new and wide open field. You can hire an online marketing firm, but I wouldn't advise it.

Two of my writers paid big bucks for this service and reported none to uneven returns. That's not to say that such companies aren't worthwhile. I'm sure many writers reap good returns from such services or they wouldn't be in business.

And I don't suggest that the companies my writers engaged (two different ones) didn't do everything they said they were going to do. It's just that at this point, selling first time, unknown writer's books online is daunting, even for marketing agents who know all the ropes.

There is an advantage the marketing companies have, of course. They know the intricacies of their trade. For you to succeed on your own, a lot depends on the extent of your expertise on the internet. It's important to the success of your book in this electronic age for you to increase your knowledge and ability in this area and call upon every aid available. If you have a knack for it, you're ahead of the game. If you don't, you can acquire the ability with determination, persistence and the help of someone with experience. Hopefully, you have a friend who can help. If not, hiring an expert to show you the ropes might not be a bad investment.

WEBSITES

Writers are advised in books and at conferences and by other writers that they must have a website, and I agree. You may not find it advantageous in the beginning, especially if you are not adept in dealing with the internet, but it's a beginning which will build in importance as you progress.

Where do you obtain a website? **For a fee**, you can have one built for you by one of the companies that specialize in this area. Lois and I had GoDaddy build ours (www.firesidepubs.com) and later, I had them build one for just the books I've published at www.firesidepublishers.com and Lois had one built at http://kadinbooks.com. We're satisfied with all three.

There are other companies. (I happened to hear of GoDaddy when I was ready for a site.) They (and I'm sure others) supply a twenty-four hour support service. The personnel are infinitely patient. If anyone can attest to this, I can. The fees assessed depend on the services you wish to purchase ranging from domain name to complete site design.
Once again, how much you contribute to maintaining your site and how much the host provider does is up to your level of expertise. I've learned gradually and now can enter my site and add or create new material. I've had a little difficulty inserting images, but I'm even conquering that problem. Remember, I'm no genius at electronics. So, again I say, if I can do it, you can do it. On the other hand, you can leave all that in the capable hands of the host if you care to do so.

Free Sites
Free websites are also available. An excellent site is www.weebly.com. This site provides tutorials for designing your page. How easy or difficult it will be for you to set the site up will depend on your level of expertise with computers. Anyone with reasonable knowledge can accomplish this by following the instructions. If you can afford it, I would advise paying the fee to have your site designed for you.

The URL's for the free sites let it be known they are indeed free. The name of the owner is included in your web address. For example, one that I might build on weebly would read:

www.firesidepublishers .weebly.com, or my name, or the title of my book, whichever I chose.

My purchased site reads:www.firesidepublishing.com. Having my own designed, paid site appears more professional. In the best of all worlds, you'll have one of each. Mark Newhouse agrees. "Every writer should fully own a personal website," he advised, "and it must be as professional as you can reasonably make it."

WEBSITE TITLE
Whichever type you chose, the title of the page is important. You want it to convey to the prospective visitor just what it is he will find there. Make it catchy, but not so catchy that one reading it will not have a clue as to what to expect from the site. Give this a lot of thought. Bounce it off a few friends. Put it aside and revisit it after a few days.

ATTRACTING TRAFFIC
The major problem you will encounter once you have your site named and up and running is how to attract "hits" or "traffic." People can't look at it if they don't know it's there. A website is something that you want people beyond your family and friends to know about, no matter how extensive your set of friends or contacts is. In Chapter Sixteen, I suggest a way to collect as many e-mail addresses as possible, but even utilizing that, to me the best answer to the problem is the use of Search Engines.

SEARCH ENGINES
A **search engine** is a 'machine' which is of utmost importance in attracting visitors to your website. In their excellent book, *The Complete Guide to Self-Publishing 4th Ed.,* Tom and Marilyn Ross note that "...18 percent of visitors find sites by search engines." That was ten years ago. There is probably a greater percentage of website visitors using search engines than ever before to locate sites of interest.

Google, Excite, Yahoo are only a few of the search engines available. You'll find many more. Check them out before signing up. All search engines charge a fee for you to be promoted. As with anything else, the services purchased will determine the cost.

KEYWORDS

Speaking of costs for services, another method of **generating traffic** to your site is through what is called "**keyword marketing.**" This is generally a 'pay-per-click' type of advertising.

You develop a list of key words or phrases you think readers will use in searching for pertinent sites. Every time someone clicks on the link to your site, you pay a small fee. There are tables on the various search engines that provide statistics on how popular the most common key words are. Be sure to check these out.

Keywords seems to be an excellent use of your advertising dollars, especially if your advertising budget is small. You know that a potential customer has visited your site because they were interested in your keyword. Even if she didn't buy your book, its title will likely remain in her mind, and she may eventually make a purchase or mention it to her friends. Just be careful that you understand how these costs can escalate.

BLOGGING

Blogging has become a popular mechanism for writing online. The best way to approach blogging is probably as an 'expert' on a particular subject. For example, if you have written a gardening book, blog about gardening. If you have written a mystery, you might want to blog about famous real mysteries of the past or about mystery writers, or a related subject. If you have written a memoir, you could pull short anecdotes from it to incorporate into your blogs.

A fairly well-known blogging address is: www.blogspot.com. Google "blogging" and you can find a list of others. A good idea is to check out other similar blogs, guest on them, before you start your own.

A GREAT BOOK ON BLOGGING:

A great book is *How to Blog a Book* by Nina Amir. This little book tells you just about everything you might want to know about blogging, especially about blogging your book, which is something I hadn't thought of doing until I read this book. Blogging may not be for everyone, and once you get into this book, and see just what it's all about, you may not want to blog your book. But in my opinion, you won't be wasting your money by purchasing this great guide. I found so much information on a subject that I really didn't know too much about that I now have to rely on self-discipline to keep from taking too much time away from writing this book to try out the interesting suggestions in Amir's book. Some of the chapter headings are: Why Blog a Book, Developing Your Blogged Book's Business Plan, Creating Your Blog, and Driving Traffic (Readers) to Your Blog. The last two chapters alone are worth the price of the book.

SOCIAL MEDIA

Facebook and Twitter have become household words in the world of social media. Is there anyone with a computer who does not have a Facebook and a Twitter account? According to just about everyone, these are must haves for authors desiring to promote their books. If you are still in the dark ages of social media, simply go to Facebook.com or Twitter.com or LinkedIn.com and proceed from there.

LinkedIn is aimed at professionals, so a non-fiction book would be at home there more so than fiction. According to

Nina Amir (see previous paragraph), "If you aren't already using social networking, start now. Do not wait."

OTHER ON-LINE PUBLICITY OPTIONS

Join and participate in chat groups. Look up online newsletters and advertise in them. Sign up for a free page somewhere like AuthorsDen.com or sign up to write short columns for a site such as hubpages.com. You are a writer. Writers have vivid imaginations. Use yours to think up a dozen other places where you can do some PR for your book.

CHAPTER SIXTEEN

VALUABLE TOOLS FOR MARKETING YOUR BOOKS

In addition to searching out venues for selling your book, you need to develop a set of tools for publicizing it. As with so many other variables in the area of marketing, you'll have to use your imagination. In this section, I will list several options you might find useful. Choose among them for the ideas that will best suit your book and your situation—or implement all of them and then see which works best for you.

FREEBEES & LOW COST

Everybody loves Freebees and inventive authors come up great, inexpensive items they can use to build good will for their book.

FREE BOOKS?

Don't be stingy with copies of your book. Check out and send copies to reviewers and to the moderators of book clubs. Check out events around town and offer a copy of the book as a door prize. Ask the host to hold the book up and say a few words about it when announcing it.

If you are trying to talk a retail store owner into displaying the book and she seems reluctant, give her a copy to read. Tell her you'll give her time to read it and come back. When you return, have everything with you to set up an exhibit of the book.

At Fireside, we give a couple of baskets of books—eight or ten different titles—to the writers' association in our state to give away at their yearly convention. We also give several hundred bookmarks for them to include in various other baskets.

You might make up a "basket" containing your book(s), bookmark and a few other items to match the theme of your book or the theme of whatever organization you are donating the basket to. For example, if it's a writing organization include items
such as markers, pens, notebooks, 3 X 5 cards—any-thing you think a writer might be able to use.

If you are donating a basket to a woman's club, you might use a chocolate theme—fill the basket with every kind of chocolate you can put your hand on and include a copy of your book.

NEWLETTERS
Write a weekly or monthly newsletter that would be of interest to people who like the genre of your book and offer to send it to them for a period of time with the purchase of the book. Or you could give it without charge, advertise your book in each issue and hope the recipient will eventually buy your book.

Newsletters would have been too expensive prior to e-mail as a promotional item because of mailing costs and paper, but now you can produce and distribute a newsletter at no monetary cost.

A word of caution here, you cannot send advertising e-mails out scattered like confetti. You can get into a lot of trouble doing that since such mass mailings may be regarded as 'spam'. You must have permission of the recipient to send such a newsletter to her, and it's never too early to begin assembling a list of e-mail addresses.

Companies exist who will manage your list for you, but they are fairly pricey. Constant Contact is one which in my experience does a good job. You can do it yourself, but remember you must get permission from the individuals on your list in order to send e-mails of this nature to them.

So, get out your clipboard. Make up a sign-up sheet with room for names, e-mail addresses and a place for the person signing to check off that she gives you permission to e-mail the newsletter to her. Carry this list with you at all times and ask everyone possible to sign it.

You can also e-mail the people now in your address book and ask for the same permission. Keep their replies in a file. Ask friends if they will ask the people in their address books for permissions as well.

I mentioned advertising your book in each issue of your newsletter, which you should do; however, don't make your newsletter one big advertisement. Be subtle. Mention the book, how it can be obtained and maybe a little about it, but don't hit the reader over the head with it.

FREE CHAPTERS OF YOUR BOOKS

Many writers have found giving away a free chapter of their book to be an effective way to get the reader's attention. If your chapter is enough of a "hook" to want someone to continue reading, you have another fan for your work and another sale.

I offer a copy of Chapter 2 of my book, *An Agent Speaks: A Primer for Unpublished Writers*. It lets the prospective reader/buyer know that the book truly does contain information useful to the unpublished writer. I will offer something from this book as soon as it's published.

If your book is non-fiction, choose a chapter which will offer the reader good information. If your book is fiction, choose a chapter—hopefully the first chapter—which will provide that "hook" mentioned above.

BUSINESS CARDS

Before you even begin to write your book, you can—and should—have business cards made up. You can probably get a good quality card at your local print shop, but you will probably get a better price—and still a quality job—from an online printer.

I've used *VISTAPRINT.com* for a few years. I've purchased cards for various uses—some with my name, some with my company's name, some with the individual titles of books that I've written or books that I've published. I've also purchased post cards and novelties such as: tote bags with an image of the cover from one of my books imprinted on it and coffee cups, also with my cover imprint.

You should know that while *VISTA* and others advertise free cards, these cards are plain or you can choose one of their designs. In order to use your logo or imprint, you will have to pay a fee; however, it is a reasonable charge and, in my opinion, worth it.

BOOKMARKS

Bookmarks are winners for you and for readers. A bookmark is an advertising method that goes on and on. Every time a reader picks up the book in which he has inserted the bookmark, he sees your book. It is hoped that sooner or later, it will lead to his buying your book.

I Googled bookmark printing and found a dozen printers listed who can fill your bookmark needs. At random, I chose www.printrunner.com. For $42.30, this shop advertised 250 2" X 6" full color one-side only bookmarks with both sides UV coated. Add $12.59 regular shipping to this and the price is still reasonable. This company ships in three business days. I noticed that some shops offered overnight service. I'm pleased with mine and plan to reorder. Other sizes are also available.

Choosing two-sided bookmarks will give you a much more handsome product and provide twice the space for your advertising message. They, of course, cost more.

Once you have the bookmarks in hand, travel as far as is reasonable to distribute them in as many retail establishments as possible. Carry some with you at all times to hand out to anyone who will take one.

One of my writers visited airports and distributed his bookmarks among books of the same genre. He reported that no one seemed to mind; however, I strongly suggest that if you want to follow this procedure—and it's a great idea to get your advertising directly into the hands of readers of your genre—you ask permission first.

POSTCARDS

Postcards can be used similarly to bookmarks. They can be handed out at various events and venues. Of course, their original purpose is for mailing and there are times when this would be useful; however, the cost of postage makes wide use of them in this way prohibitive. One advantage over bookmarks is the size. You can easily insert an image of the cover of you book on a postcard. Or you can be inventive: e.g. Olive Church puts photos of herself in her pink dress and boa on her cards.

NOVELTIES

Remember those tote bags and coffee cups I mentioned? They're pricey, too much so to hand out indiscriminately, but you might consider them for special occasions. For example, if you decide to give book parties, one would be nice for a hostess gift.

Joan West

Carry a tote with your book's image on it yourself. Everyone who sees you will also see it. If your day job is in an office and you keep your own coffee cup there, switch to one with an image of your book cover on it.

You can also purchase pens with an imprint on them in lots of 100 from several companies. They're not too expensive this way and I've found it a way to keep myself in pens also

SIGNATURE LINES
Don't forget something as simple as including the words, "Author of The Title of Your Book" plus your website address, or some indication of where your book can be obtained, under your name on your computer e-mail or on any snail mail that you send out. If you are offering a free newsletter or chapters of your book, you can note that here also.

ENDORSEMENTS: BLURBS

The right sorts of endorsements can help sell your book. Gather them whenever you can, but remember an endorsement from your Aunt Sally won't help, not unless she is a well-known writer.

The better known the endorser, the more weight the endorsement will carry. Of course, the endorser must have some connection to the book—a writer who has published traditionally, if well-known so much the better; a veterinarian, if your book is about animals; a chef, if your book is about cooking.

If you have two or three of the above, it's okay to include a self-published writer, but generally speaking, it's better to go without endorsement than to list a group of writers who may well be very good writers, but who have no platform to support them.

On the other hand, while most traditionally published books have one to seven endorsements, Nina Amir lists an even dozen for her *How to Blog a Book*, so many she had to list them on two pages inside the book rather than on the back cover. Her list includes such well-known writers in the field of publishing as Dan Poynter, Jeff Herman and Shel Horowitz.

Let's suppose that you don't know anyone who is well known. Does that mean you should give up and go without endorsements? You can, and many first books do, debut without them; however, ways do exist to obtain good endorsements.

You can send your galleys to a few authors who write in your field and request an endorsement. You may not get one, but then again, you may.

You also can send the galleys to reviewers. Look for those that are interested in your genre. You lose nothing except a galley for trying.

If you have to go without endorsements on the cover of your book, don't feel bad. When your book becomes a success, you can thumb your nose at those people who forfeited the chance to have their names associated with a bestselling book.

YOUR PRESS KIT

A press kit is a package that you will send out to media sources. It's a wonderful tool for clarifying and educating the recipient about your book. In order to do that, it will consist of several well-designed pages of information and images always available to send out at a moment's notice to a likely recipient.

Marketing guru, Linda terBurg has dotted all the i's and crossed all the t's in her workbook which clearly lays out complete instructions regarding the development of a press kit.

In her book, *HOW TO SELL YOUR BOOKS: WORKBOOK*, Linda lists the five major pieces of a press kit:
- the press release,
- the pitch letter
- the author bio
- a picture of your book's front cover
- 10 talking questions with answers.

She goes into each of these elements in depth. She includes copies of the actual pitch letter, press release, author bio, author photo, an image of the book's front and back covers and a list of ten questions with answers.

This is an incredible book about an incredible book launch. It is, as noted above, a workbook. As such, it includes check lists, lists for you the writer to fill in the blank and a reading list. "I want you to start reading now," she says. "...but first, you need to read (my book) from cover to cover."

The development of a press kit should begin even before you start writing, if possible. Many of the elements are those you will use outside the kit, time and time again. You will be sending your press release out on its own many, many times, as you will your author's bio and your pitch letter. This last will be tweaked to suit the particular recipient each time you send it out, but the basic letter will remain essentially the same.

A NEWS RELEASE

Today what once was called a press release, is known as a news release. Press indicates print media, news includes all media.

Your news release must include *all* pertinent information—book title, author's name, name of publisher, website, name of contact person and his e-mail address, telephone number and mailing address.

In a news release, a clever title and tight copy writing are unbeatable assets. The title should—here's that word again—"hook" the newspaper editor's curiosity (or that of whatever other important person is reading it). Editors are inundated with news releases every day. Make yours stand out or it will immediately be tossed without a second look.

Now that you have her attention, write tight copy. You only have a page and you have a lot of information to impart on it. Tell enough about the book to intrigue her. Tell enough about you, the author, to make yourself interesting. Include your platform credentials, if relevant.

Keep in mind that some newspaper editors will drop your news release onto the page with little or no editing. In fact, to enhance your chances of getting your information onto the pages of the newspaper, write it to read like a short article. Write tight. Write like a journalist. Give the editor the who, what, where, when, why of journalism and she will love you.

Conclude with information of where the book may be purchased. Get it in, but soft pedal it. The newspaper is not in the business of giving away a lot of free advertising, but

done gently you can get by with it. In fact, the editor expects it. Just don't hit her in the face with it.
Attach a second page with the statistics of the book. (See the Appendix for an example.)

This release may also be sent to others, to independent booksellers around the country, for example, to whom you can then ship orders for your book via media mail.

In your search for presentation dates, you might send it to the program chairs of organizations along with a copy of the book. If your cover is impressive—and I assume it is—you might want to insert a small image, perhaps on the statistics page if you can't find room on the front page.

CONTESTS

Mark Newhouse notes that another way to build a name for yourself is through contests for writing and for your books. I second that suggestion wholeheartedly.

Mark knows whereof he speaks as he has won several contests among them his *Rockhound Science Mystery Series* with a CD Rom won the Teacher's Choice Award from Learning Magazine in 2001. Another of his books, *The Midnight Diet Club*, (formerly *You Never See Fat Vampires,*) took first prize in the Young Adult (YA) category from the Florida Writers' Association in 2011. This book is a good example of the answer to the question, "Why do you write?" raised in Chapter Two. The act of bullying is something that Mark detests, not only as a human being, but as a teacher. Giving thought to what is a popular theme for today's young people, he came up with vampires as an analogy to bullies. Putting that together with his writing skills and his passion for the subject, Mark came up with a winner.

Mark advocates not waiting for a first book to enter contests, but to enter contests for short stories, poems and others in an effort to build credentials and your platform. Yet another award for this writer was the Editor's Choice Award for his story, *The Warehouse*, which appeared in *The Second Annual Journal of the Creative Writers Notebook,* which grew out of a newsletter called The Notebook. As the editor of the newsletter at that time, I am aware of how this writer built his platform one brick at a time and recently was a winner in the Writer's Digest short story competition, the Florida Writer's Association competitions and others.

You can do it too. As Olive Church says, "The goal is *not* only just to sell books: The bottom line, the ultimate purpose is to get your name known!"

You can find lists of contests everywhere. Most writers' newsletters (see Appendix for several of these) list current contests and that old faithful, *Writer's Market* devotes an entire section to them, as does the monthly *Writer's Digest Magazine*. So compile a list and begin submitting to them. Some are free, many charge a fee. Many are contests for novels, published or unpublished; many are for short stories. If you don't write short stories, look through your novel's manuscript. You may be able to adapt a chapter to a short story. Mark points out, "Don't be discouraged if you don't win. Being a finalist is also a credit you can add to your credentials."

One e-newsletter that I like is Writer Gazette. It comes from Canada and its owner, Krista Barrett says: "We provide writers worldwide with a resource site that provides tips, techniques, resources, articles, job postings, and more to help induce, improve, and promote a writing career." This newsletter is free to the public. (See Appendix for contact information.)

173

Joan West

As noted at the beginning of the chapter, these are some of the tools you can use to promote and sell your book. You may think of others. If you do, let me know. I'm always looking for good tools and new ones are always appreciated. In fact, if you send a useful one, I'll include it and cite you, when I update this book in the future!

Many people think of writing as a solitary experience, but just as I asked for your help a moment ago, we all benefit from networking and learning from others. Let's take a quick look at some of the helpful resources you may want to explore.

CHAPTER SEVENTEEN

<u>YOU ARE NOT ALONE</u>
<u>HELP!!!</u>

Many people thing of writing as a solitary experience, but I have found we all need and benefit from networking and learning from others.

Writing groups, associations, coaches and books on all aspects of writing -each plays a different and important role in a writer's life. Let's take a look at each of them separately and see how they could be of use to you.

BOOKS: GREAT RESOURCES

Such a wealth of written material is available to writers today. Mention any specific area and you can find a book written especially for it—writing and selling your first novel, writing for children, finding an agent, grammar and punctuation, marketing—the list seems endless.

If you thought the idea of someone publishing a book about "writing a book in a month" was astonishing, how about the one mentioned in Chapter Sixteen, *How to Blog a Book?* by Nina Amir, author and—what else—a blogger. A blogger? Unheard of just a few years ago, but books help even us older authors keep up.

But if you're not a blogger and are just looking for information on how to write or how to get an agent or how to self-publish or how to market your book or seventeen other how-to questions, go no farther than your local bookstore or online to www.Writers Digest Books.com and be amazed by the variety of these resources that 'keep you from reinventing the wheel."

All those 'unprofessional', doomed queries that I've received and continue to receive are completely unnecessary if potential authors just crack open a good book.

As a writer, you should have a bookcase filled with professionally written resource books, beginning with the best dictionary you can afford and a copy of *Roget's Thesaurus*. This won't bust your budget. And don't forget the classic, Strunk and White's The Elements of Style. Both my Roget's and my Strunk & White's cost me under four dollars each, which will give you an idea of how long I've had them. Of course, the *University of Chicago Stylebook* is probably the one most used by publishers today. It's pricy, but your library may have a copy.

After you have these basic texts, begin to build your writing library with books like *Edit Yourself* and if you are going to self-publish, you need at least one of the several excellent books in that field (see Appendix). Then go from there for titles of specific interest to you, including a good marketing book. Two of my favorites in this category are Rob Eagar's *Sell Your Book like Wildfire: The Writer's Guide to Marketing & Publicity, and the aforementioned How to Sell Your Books Workbook by Linda terBurg, and How to Sell Your Books Checklist by Mark H Newhouse.* The Workbook and the Checklist books encourage you to put your goals, plans and options down in writing. If you see them staring you in the face, you're more likely to act on them and achieve success.

So many good books are out there, I couldn't possibly name them all. I tried to list as many as I could think of in the Appendix. Take a look and, as soon as you've finished reading this book, take yourself to a bookstore and begin or add to your collection.

WRITER'S GROUPS

Writer's groups can be incredibly helpful to a writer. These groups come in all shapes and sizes. Some are for professionals only, some are for poets, some for fiction writers, some for beginners, the list goes on.

One of our local groups caters to fantasy and horror writers. Its moderator, Jim McGann, was kind enough to share the following about the benefits of belonging to a critique group:

"To me the benefits of belonging to writing groups in general include the following:

- The camaraderie of other individuals interested in the craft of writing.

- Assistance in conquering any innate shyness by reading your work to others.

- The increased awareness of awkward writing that only comes from reading your work aloud.

- The possibility of improving your art by receiving impartial and constructive feed-back.

- The improvement in your own writing that comes from critiquing the writing of others

In addition to the preceding, there are other benefits to belonging to a writing group dedicated to a particular genre which is your main love. Three of these leap to mind:

- Working with other individuals who share your enthusiasm for the type of stories that you write.

• Listening/reading the very type of material that is most enjoyable to you.

• Receiving even more astute critiques from members who are familiar with the conventions of that type of material."

Jim's group is genre specific, but there are many groups that encourage you to explore different forms of writing.

One such group is The Villages Creative Writer's Group which welcomes any writer who writes anything at all. Beginners, self-published writers and professionals are all welcome. My husband, Glen West, moderated this group for fourteen years and says, "Belonging to a writing group encourages you to write—to put your thoughts on paper. The members of the group can be helpful in their critiques of sentence structure, grammar, punctuation and dialog."

The encouragement or motivation to write is a key component of a writer's group. Many of us are procrastinators at best and lazy at worse. The writing group may help by making us feel we have a deadline we have to meet.

WRITER'S ASSOCIATIONS

Writer's associations differ from writing groups in several ways. Writer's associations are larger than writing groups. Associations are sometimes statewide, sometimes regional, sometimes for specific groups of writers, such as the association for the Romance Writers of America (RWA).

An association accepts individual writers as members of the "mother" group, but often sponsors smaller writing groups located throughout the area they represent. The Florida Writers Association (FWA) is not limited to writers from

Florida. Although, most members do reside in the sunshine state, many are scattered through the country and I'm told they even have one member outside of the United States, which makes them international in scope!

Chrissy Jackson, President of FWA explains it better than I do:

> "There are various types of writers associations and their purposes are usually spelled out in the forming documents. For us, we are a 501[c]6 which is a trade association. That means we represent all areas of writing, illustrating, publishing, marketing, and everything connected to writing in everything we do. This colors our membership outreach, our conference planning, our mini-conference topics, and the Writers Group speakers. We encourage participation from all angles, and work hard to make sure our members are exposed to improving their craft, various types of publishing and kept abreast of all things writing.
>
> Some other writer's associations are only focused on writing and publishing, some only on publishing, some only on illustrating. That narrows their intent, their purpose, and consequently their membership. Our Critique Groups across the state and online exist to improve our members' writing for their benefit. Some of our members write for their own pleasure, never wanting to be published. A true trade association, such as Florida Writers Association, exists to provide resources for our members in all areas of the literary world.

Joan West

She goes on to explain some of the benefits:

> Writing is scary, intimidating to some,
> overwhelming to others, and getting published
> even more so. The value of FWA is to help all
> members find the resources they need to take
> their writing to the level they want, and to do
> it in a friendly, non-confrontational way that
> reinforces the family values and themes at
> FWA's core. We are a group of hard-working
> folks who care about the written word, but
> care more about writers and their personal
> growth.

She concludes by the most important benefit:

> Our bylaws attest to the organizational
> structure, but our motto says it all: Writers
> Helping Writers.

FWA is certainly a good fit for this book and its publishing company, whose mission is: Helping Writers Succeed.

In addition to what Chrissy has shared with us, FWA like most other associations, maintains an online book store where members may offer their books for sale. Also, during the yearly conference, members may sell their books on the conference site.

Let's look at another state Association:

On their informative website, The Michigan Writer's Association explains why a writer should join their group by suggesting that members may "...attend free craft, publishing, and marketing workshops and member potluck." You can also submit your work to their Chapbook contest, receive a subscription to their Dunes Review and stay up to date regarding upcoming literary events in Northern Michigan. Members may also "...apply for scholarships to select writers conferences and retreats." The cost for all this, when I looked, was only $40 a year.

I would say joining an association is a real bargain, when you consider enjoying the company, moral support and motivation of other authors. Look for an association in your area and join it right away.

CLASSES

Just as a writing group motivates and challenges a writer, so too do writing classes. These are offered in a variety of venues.
In my community, we have a Lifelong Learning College. The instructors are not necessarily teacher certified in any subject, but bring considerable experience to their classrooms. Some, as in my case, have had formal teaching experience, but the classes they offer may be on different subjects entirely than what they taught in their career. Teaching such courses may be another fun way to build your platform.

Before retiring, I taught sociology and psychology in colleges; however, in the local Lifelong Learning College I taught a number of course for writers about agents and publishing. Several other instructors came from various backgrounds but amassed great knowledge of writing or publishing which they were also generously sharing by conducting classes.

Check out your community. If there is no formal adult educational organization such as ours, call the high school. Frequently, various classes are taught in the evening adult learning sections. Some colleges offer this non-credit service also.

How about going back to class yourself? Sharpen your skills, update your knowledge by attending a class on writing, publishing or marketing. If there is a college in your area and it doesn't offer this type of class, ask about auditing a regular college class. This is simple: you pay the fee, attend all the classes, do the assignments, but receive no credit. What you do receive are the latest updates in the information you need to become the best at your chosen field.

A warning: Ask around. See if you can find a few people who have taken the course. Ask them for feedback. You don't want to be in the shoes of a couple of writers I know, who took a writing class offered in their locality and discovered the instructor to be less than qualified.

WRITING COACHES

I've had a number of writers ask if they should hire a writing coach?

Jamie Morris is a writing coach with the Woodstream Writers in Orlando, Florida. I asked Jamie to tell us a little about why it would be beneficial for a writer to hire a coach. Her helpful reply follows:

> *The best writing coach is one who is on your side! Collaborative and well-informed, she should invest herself in the success of your work, empowering you while helping you evaluate concepts, develop themes, and create a voice that both suits your material and engages your readers.*
>
> *Pointing out both what is working and what is not, your writing coach gives you complete support at every point along your writer's journey. From the earliest brainstorming*

sessions all the way to the completion of your final draft, your coach offers you custom-tailored strategies to keep your work heading to 'The End.

You can find this information and more on her website, (www.WoodstreamWriters.com).

Remember, with the availability of e-mail and the use of attachments, you and your coach, editor, agent or book doctor can be miles, even states or countries apart.

BOOK DOCTORS

Bobbie Christmas, book doctor and author of *Write In Style, Purge Your Prose of Problems,* and other books for writers, established Zebra Communications in 1992. From metro Atlanta, she edits books for publishing houses and individuals around the globe. Bobbie belongs to and works with FWA. She also contributes a column to the newsletter, the *Creative Writer's Notebook (see Appendix).* I asked her to tell my readers just what it is a book doctor does. Read on.

I've been an editor for forty years, and for the past twenty, I've specialized as a book doctor. For decades now, folks have asked me, "What's a book doctor, and why would I need one?

First, imagine you need a flu shot. For such a simple medical issue, you can drop by any place giving flu shots, from a "doc-in-the-box" to a supermarket pharmacy, where a nurse will give you your injection. When you feel sick, though, you see a physician, one with extensive training. Unlike a nurse, a physician gives you a thorough physical exam, from head to toe. He or she checks your vital signs, listens to your heart and lungs, and looks deeply into your ears, nose, and throat. A doctor gets to know all about patients before diagnosing, medicating, and monitoring them.

The same setup applies to the literary world. Everyone should get a flu shot, and every book must be edited before it gets published, but the same as when you need a simple flu shot, simple books intended for a limited audience, such as a family history, may need only a line editor. Line editors treat only the most immediate issues, such as errors in grammar and punctuation. If you have bigger hopes for your book—finding an agent or marketing it to a broad audience—or if you have any concerns that your book needs a little help in any area, a book doctor will not only correct the grammar and punctuation, but will also perform a thorough exam of all the elements of the book and make recommendations to cure the book's ills.

A word of warning: an English teacher may appear to be a good person to edit a book, and a teacher will catch errors in grammar, but when it comes to punctuation and capitalization, most teachers are familiar with academic style, which schools prefer, whereas book doctors are intimately familiar with Chicago style, the style of punctuation, capitalization, and formatting that book publishers prefer. Book doctors also perform developmental editing—sometimes called concept editing. In-depth editing not only addresses grammar and punctuation; it includes an evaluation of all the elements, such as organization, pacing, clarity, and *creativity. With fiction, book doctors also examine the plot, characterization, dialogue, voice, and more. Book doctors also catch unclear or awkward sentences, delete redundancies, reduce wordiness, and address many other flaws that may not be technical errors, so a line editor would not fix them. Most book doctors also write an evaluation that makes further suggestions and gives you tips on how to make your book the very best it can be. Again, a line editor repairs the most immediate technical errors, while a book doctor delves deeper and cures whatever ails a manuscript.*

As a book doctor, my mission is to do everything possible to help clients produce marketable manuscripts. As a result, I've saved clients embarrassment and possible rejection. For example, in a children's book I edited, a giant daddy longlegs spider threw a web around a character. A typical editor probably would not question such an event, as long as the grammar was correct. In actuality, though, daddy longlegs spiders don't produce silk or spin webs, and even though the story was a fantasy, a knowledgeable publisher would never let a scientific flaw appear in a book. In another book, a sand crab crawls sideways across a beach. Sand crabs, though, do not crawl sideways like most other crabs; they can move only backwards, and they rarely show themselves. They tend to burrow into the sand at the water's edge and disappear. In another novel, the protagonist belonged to a popular band. Unfortunately the author had selected a name of a band that was already popular, and such usage could get the author in legal trouble. Whoops! Bobbie the book doctor to the rescue! A book doctor, while not expected to be a fact checker or an attorney, should know enough to tell the author when to check facts and/or avoid potential legal issues.

We all have pet words and phrases, so another thing that authors rarely see in their own work is their own repetition. A good book doctor will spot it and make suggestions for removal.

We cannot know what we don't know. We can't see what we've become too accustomed to seeing. A book doctor offers a fresh set of eyes as well as a fresh and professional perspective on every aspect of your manuscript.

To sum up, if you never plan to sell your book— if you've written it only for your family and friends—you may need only a line editor, one who will catch errors in grammar and punctuation. If you have high hopes for your fiction or nonfiction book and want to self- publish it or sell it to a publisher, you need a book doctor. A book doctor delves into every detail of the manuscript and makes sure your book is healthy and strong enough to reach its full potential.

Now you have the real deal directly from the pen (computer?) of a real book doctor. They don't come cheap, so I hope this has helped you to understand exactly what you can expect. In my opinion, if it fits your pocketbook, it's worth it.

FREELANCE/INDEPENDENT EDITORS

I had asked Tom Wallace, a freelance writer with over fourteen years of writing and editing experience in the corporate world for some advice to include in my prior book, *An Agent Speaks*. What he said then is every bit as appropriate today. His suggestions for writers were and are: "Approach the editing process as a learning experience. A good writer/editor relationship can do more than make your current book ready for publication. It can help you to hone your craft—to get to the next plateau in your writing."

Wallace says, "Work with your editor. Don't just sit back and wait for feedback. Be involved in the process. Ask questions about why the editor wants certain changes. It's even okay to disagree with your editor. But listen to his or her reasoning first, and make sure you have a good reason of your own for doing it your way.

"Find a freelance editor who '*gets*' your writing. Someone may be highly educated, have years of experience, and be professionally well-respected. That doesn't mean he or she will hear your voice. Get sample edits from a few," Wallace concludes, "and go with the one who responds to your work in the most enlightened way."

MORAL OF THE STORY:
You don't need to do it all on your own. Just like you have turned to this book for help, there are lots of books, and generous folk who want to help you. And who knows, someday, when you are a famous author, you may be willing to repay the favor and help other wannabe writers too.

CHAPTER EIGHTEEN

A FEW WORDS ABOUT WRITING

It wouldn't seem right to conclude a book for authors about publishing without talking about writing itself.

BEGIN AT THE BEGINNING

I've mentioned in prior chapters the importance of beginning at the beginning. The reader doesn't need to know—doesn't *want* to know at this point—what led up to the immediate course of action— the *background* of the story. A novel needs to have a problem at its core and it's important to set that problem up, no matter how discreetly, at the beginning. That's your hook and you need it to make the reader want to turn the page.

Before going further, let me dismiss any notion that I am a writing instructor. I am not. What I include in this chapter is information I have gleaned throughout my career as writer, agent and publisher in addition to what successful writers have been kind enough to contribute to the book.

HINTS FROM THE PROS

Bobbie Christmas, who generously shared the role of the book doctor with us in the previous chapter, published a book, *Purge Your Prose of Problems: A Book Doctor's Desk Reference,* which unfortunately is now out of print; however at this moment, a few copies remain. If any are left as you read this, I would recommend it to every writer. The following two examples taken directly from the book are the kinds of things every writer can use. The advice in the first could have come straight from the mouth of Ernest Hemingway.

Action scenes should be tight

Good action scenes quicken our heart rate with fast-paced writing. In action scenes, cut each sentence to essential information, to pick up the pace. No extraneous wording should detract from the action. In action scenes, delete or shorten descriptions, keep adjectives and adverbs to a minimum, and choose powerful verbs.

Every day/Everyday

Every day: Each day. *We milk the cows every day.*
Everyday: Ordinary, commonplace, routine. *We wear everyday clothes when we perform our chores.*

If all copies are gone by the time you read this, you might try to obtain a copy for a reasonable price from half.com. I hope that Bobbie will reconsider and put this valuable tool back into print or, barring that, some other enterprising editor or book doctor will publish a similar guide. Are you listening Writer's Digest Books?

Bonnie Trenga is the author of the cleverly titled book, *The Curious Case of the Misplaced Modifier: How to Solve the Mysteries of Weak Writing*. A small (five by seven-and-a-half) hard cover book, the information Trenga shares with her readers is presented clearly and concisely. You'll find comparisons, exercises and recaps between its pages. One chart, for example sports these headings: Wordy Phrase; Wordy Sentence; How to Rewrite; and Concise Sentence. You can't go wrong with this kind of clarity.

The book covers passive voice, weak verbs— worth the price for this chapter alone—and "*ing*" words along with the illusive misplaced modifier.

I count passive voice as one of the biggest mistakes made by first time writers. Trenga uses examples such as:

Passive - The hot dog vendor was bitten by the sausage seller.

Active - The sausage seller bit the hot dog vender.

Not to be one-sided, she then illustrates when it's okay to use passive voice.

Trenga says the use of "ing" words creates vague sentences. Get rid of them and your sentences become clear. I might add that it also messes with your syntax. Take a look at this example from Trenga's book:

"The officer realized some vital evidence had gotten lost while eating lunch." What? The vital evidence was eating lunch?

By restructuring the sentence you straighten out your syntax and create a specific, clear sentence.

Trenga's rewrite: "While the officer was eating lunch, he realized he'd lost some vital evidence."

I guarantee you will find a writing no-no that you indulge in within these pages. It's a handy little book.

Another favorite of mine is **Theodore A. Rees Cheney's** *Getting the Words Right: How to Rewrite, Edit & Revise,* which covers three of the most important aspects of writing.

Unbelievably, I once received a manuscript with an accompanying letter that declared, "I never rewrite. I feel that my first thoughts are spontaneous and therefore the best." I don't think I've ever read such sloppily written material. Of course, I only read the first paragraph in deference to my blood pressure.

Incidentally, Max Perkins, Hemingway's editor, noted that the great writer tended to overcorrect himself. By the writer's own count, he rewrote A Farewell to Arms over fifty times!

Back to Cheney, I love this heading of his: Which *Which* is *That*? Then these: Lesser Reductions; Redundancy; The reason was because; Circumlocation; Authorial Intrusion; Short for Long; Pleonasm; and Prolixity—all in Chapter 1. Do you recognize pleonasm and prolixity? Fess up now. I had to look them up.

Simply said, pleonasm is "the error of saying essentially the same thing again in the same sentence" and prolixity is "A form of verbosity, prolixity means the mention of things not worth mentioning."

Cheney obviously likes to have fun with words, but his book is a keeper. It's the proverbial gold mine of information to which every writer needs to have access.

In a recent article for the McClatchy Newspapers, **James A. Fussell** asks the question, "...whom really cares...?" Fussell is referring, of course, to the use of "who" versus "whom." He suggests that it was important to Ernest Hemingway. *To Who the Bell Tolls* doesn't have quite the punch as *To Whom* in the book's title. Otherwise the correct use of the pronouns is up for grabs today. As Fussell points out, a movie titled "*I Married Whom*" or dialog such as, "Who is it?" "It is I," sounds stupid or at least cringingly British."

I agree. As that last sentence suggests, another pair of pronouns used incorrectly is "me" and "I". Do you know of a writer who wouldn't write, "It's me" in the above situation? Or who would write, "She's in the tenth grade like me" in spite of the fact that in both cases, "I" is the proper pronoun to use? However, the use of proper grammar in your writing should be the rule rather than the exception.

TIME IS A PAIN IN A WRITER'S ...SCHEDULE

Along with everything else we do, time usage rears its ugly head for writers. How much time do you use daily checking your e-mail or your Facebook or Twitter pages? I'd bet it's too much. I struggle with this problem and I'm sure that most other writers do also.

Time is a writer's most important commodity. The one thing writing takes is *time*. Hopefully, you've developed the discipline to set aside a certain time for your writing. Ideally, it will be a reasonable length of time for you to accomplish a decent number of pages. In fact, some writers set a number of pages to complete as opposed to a time limit.

However you do it, make it something reasonably doable. If you set your goal for too long a time or too many pages, you will fail to achieve your goal and your writing schedule will be chaotic and you not only will frustrate yourself, you won't get any work done.

As for those pesky e-mails and Facebook and Twitter pages, don't include them in your writing schedule. Set aside an entirely separate time schedule for them. I don't let myself look at anything online until I have accomplished my writing goal for the day.

To establish this 'habit' took a great deal of discipline and I didn't succeed overnight, but now it's not so difficult and has made a tremendous difference in the amount of pages I am able to turn out per day.

WRITER'S BLOCK

A chapter on writing 'demons' wouldn't be complete without a mention of "writer's block." This affects each writer differently and the best suggestion I can make came from Ernest Hemingway, who said that he always stopped his day's writing knowing what the next sentence in his manuscript would be.

What better advice could you have?

PUNCTUATION

Remember in Chapter Seven when writer Allen Watkins mentioned that comma usage has changed since he went to school? I agree with that assessment and I admit that punctuation has always been a challenge for me. I'm sure that is the case with many writers, so I want to conclude this chapter on writing by recommending Noah Lukeman's *A Dash of Style: The Art and mastery of Punctuation*. I think it's safe to say that just about anything you want to know about punctuation you will find in this book.

I won't try to quote from it. There's just too much information, but his Contents page says it all:

Part 1 addresses what he calls The Triumvirate: the Period (the Stop Sign), The Comma (the Speed Bump) and The Semicolon (the Bridge).

Part 2, he calls Into the Limelight: The Colon (the Magician, The Dash and Parentheses (the Interrupter and the Advisor), The Quotation Marks (the Trumpets) and The Paragraph and Section Breaks (the Stoplight and the Town Line).

Part 3 warns the writer to Proceed with Caution describing The Question Mark, Exclamation Point, Italics, Points of Ellipsis, and the Hyphen.

Isn't that an example of a marvelous imagination, not to mention covering all the bases? Lukeman even treats us to an Epilogue: the Symphony of Punctuation.

Our last chapter lays out some of the necessities required for the *business* of writing, but this is the end of what I hope have been chapters filled with information that will help you write your way to your goal, whatever that is. I'd love to hear from you along the way.

CHAPTER 19

WRITING IS A BUSINESS

Just as writers are seldom natural marketers, so they are seldom natural businessmen, but as with marketing, it's something a serious writer must learn.
Whether you like it or not, writing is a business—that is if you sell your product.

TAXES

Notice, I said, if you sell your product. I didn't say, if you make any money from your writing. The minute you make a sale, you're in business and you are required to register with your state's sales tax authority and you or your tax person must file at least a Schedule "C" with your Federal Income Tax form.

Because of this, when you first put pen to paper or fingers to the keyboard, it is essential that you keep track of any expenditures that relate to your writing.

These will include the pen, paper, keyboard and computer. All of these will be deducted from the money you receive from sales of your book and the remainder will be your profit on which you must pay taxes. If you spend more than you take in, you may deduct that amount from your personal income tax.

Be aware that whether you make a profit or not, you must file these two taxes—unless you live in Delaware where there is no sales tax.

When I first started, I was burned when I failed to submit a sales tax form for a quarter during which I had no profit. No profit, no tax, I thought. Right, but the state requires that a form be submitted regardless and I was fined $50 for my carelessness.

The county you live in may have some kind of business tax and your city may require a license of some kind. Be sure you explore all the avenues so your business will be legal.

WHAT'S LEGAL?

I'm not an attorney, so I can't tell you what is legal and what is not. In my opinion, it's a good idea to have an attorney to consult when you have questions in this area; however, I realize that legal services are fairly expensive. If you can't or don't want to go that route, at least get a good book, one that will keep you up on the basics.

The one that I have is called *Law (in plain English) for Writers*. Its contents are extensive. Separated into three parts:

Section I deals with "The Writer's Words" (defamation, copyright, etc.).

Section II discusses "The Writer's Relationships" (publishers, agents, contracts, etc.)

Section III expands on what you will learn in this chapter. It's titled, The Writer's Business dealing with writing as a business, taxes, your estate, etc.

Another interesting book is Tad Crawford's *Business and Legal Forms for Authors and Self-Publishers*. This book discusses contracts and lawyers in addition to providing copies of 25 different forms that a writer might need during her career. The book also comes with a cd containing the forms for you to utilize.

INCORPORATE?

Another legal issue is whether or not to incorporate yourself. I found a book by Judith H. McQuown entitled, *Inc. Yourself: How to Profit by Setting up Your Own Corporation,* very helpful. *Honestly, this is a tough question.*

I'm sure there are times when incorporating as a writer would be beneficial to the individual author. I thought at one time that it would be useful to incorporate Lois' and my literary agency and I did so. On further consideration, we decided that it really wasn't the way to go for us, and I "unincorporated" us. As I said, it isn't an easy decision so you need to look into it carefully. It might be a good fit for you, but not for us.
Other forms of ownership for your business are sole Proprietorship or partnership. Check them all out before you decide.

FICTITIOUS NAME AND BANK ACCOUNT

Don't forget that you will need a separate bank account for your business. Unless you plan to use your name as the name of the business—and I don't advise it—you will need to have a fictitious name recorded with your state government. The cost will vary by state. I believe mine cost $50. Don't forget that it needs to be renewed periodically.

You will use this fictitious name for your web- site, so be sure the name you choose has not already been used as a website or e-mail address.

DAY TO DAY OPERATIONS

As I mentioned under "Taxes," earlier in this chapter, it's essential that you become a good bookkeeper. You must form the habit of keeping track of our income and expenditures.

Set up a system for yourself so that at the end of the month, or the quarter, or the year, everything will be set out in black and white for you. (Hopefully "red" will not enter the picture.) Your records will reflect what you spend on things large and small from the purchase of a computer or printer to utilities to postage and paper.

Be thorough, be accurate and keep all receipts.

HANDLING THE PRODUCT

Your book is your product. You must place orders for it with your printer. You must decide how you will take orders for sales. You must decide what discounts you will offer. You must determine how you will fulfill the orders (ship the books). You must decide what you will do about returns. You must set up an invoicing system. You must keep track of inventory. You must have a system for recording income and one for recording expenditures.

If you can afford to hire someone to do these chores for you, so much the better; if you can't, expect to tear out your hair or let out a scream now and then.

I know, you're a writer, not a bookkeeper, but someone has to do it. I would suggest setting up a schedule—a couple of hours per week or a day a month, for example.

Whatever you do, don't throw the paperwork in a drawer to do when you have time. You'll never have time and when tax times come, you'll be in a very bad position.

PRICING YOUR PRODUCT

Ah, here is a most important decision for your pocketbook. The product must not cost you more than your profit when you sell it. You must factor in all expenses before you can price your book. For various reasons, different writers may have different expenditures to account for; however, most are standard.

The cost per book to have it printed comes immediately to your mind, but that's only the beginning.

Every penny you spend in the process of getting to the actual printing must be included, such as paying for editing, paying for help in designing your cover, any help you paid for in bringing your story from manuscript to book form.

As I mentioned in "Taxes," keep and record all those pesky little receipts for pencils and paper and glue sticks, along with the ones for the major purchases: computers, printers and the like. All of this comes under the heading of "Overhead." Every book you print must assume its share of Overhead.

How do you figure that? Add up all of your overhead expenses and divide by the number of books you have printed for sale. This will be slightly off depending on how many you give away. If you want to be on the penny, you will have to have that figure to deduct from the total number of books printed.

How much are you spending for advertising? How much are you spending for developing your website? How much are you spending for shipping?

When you set out to determine the sale price you will assign to your book, all of these costs play a part in your decision. With this in mind, let's take a look at the idea of your using a national distributor in order to get your book into a major bookstore.

Joan West

Let's say you want to sell your book for $13.95. The distributor, who takes 55 percent of the retail price, will pay you $6.28 for every copy he sells.

What do you have to deduct from that amount? It's share of the overhead (all the items mentioned above probably plus some others), the cost to print one book and the cost to ship the book.

But wait, what happens when the distributor returns the book to you at a shipping cost of $7.43. Where are you now?

Well, let's see. Let's assume it cost you $3.50 (I'm estimating here) to print the book plus the cost of shipping the book to you and the cost of shipping the book to the distributor, say $1.50 (Shipping a single book would cost more ($2.47), but I'm assuming you are shipping more than one at a time, making the total per book less.) which comes to a total of $5. Let's assume that your overhead per book is $0.58. If so, you make $0.70 for your book! But if any of the above figures (print, shipping or overhead) are larger than my estimates, you're in the red.

Remember, I've pulled those three figures out of my head. Yours may differ significantly. Run *your* numbers. It's critical for your "bottom line" that you run the figures and be sure to include everything; however, don't be discouraged. You may be willing to take this loss for a couple of reasons. There is a silver lining.

Getting your book into the major bookstores gives you some prestige. It also helps to get your name and the title of your book more known. But the point that will make it okay to take a loss here, is that the royalty from your book in e-book form can make up for the loss from your distributor. We can also hope that you will be making a profit of some sort from the books you are selling on your own.

So, national distribution, if you can get it, may be worthwhile, but you need to fully evaluate your tolerance for loss. Your other sales should make up for your loss there; however, sometimes without this distribution, your profit will be greater.

Important: In every case, run the figures for *your* book and see what the bottom line is before setting your prices.

Obviously publishing a book is much more involved than "just" the writing of it. I've heard many writers say that the writing is the easy part. You can see that in self-publishing you have taken on a myriad of tasks. Get started. Carve out time to make a plan today.

MY CONCLUSION = YOUR BEGINNING

Well, that's it. I've tried to put down everything I could think of, everything I've learned from my experiences as a teacher, an agent and a publisher that I thought might help you achieve the dream of becoming an author. As I said at the beginning, this book, like every other, can't possibly cover every aspect of this wonderful, but complicated 'business' I love so you still must do your homework and seek out help from others. I hope I have helped you achieve your goals as a writer. I welcome your comments and ideas and wish you unbounded success in your writing career. Thank you for allowing me to share my story with you.

Joan West,
Lady Lake, Florida

APPENDIX

Resources

Editors, Writing Coaches and Book Doctors:

Suzy Allegra
Writing Coach
Life Coach
www.suzyallegra.com
602-531-3929

Martha Jeffers
The Grammar Granny
Copy Editing-Proofreading-Typing
Motivational Speaking
1703-4 Park Meadows Drive
Fort Myers, Florida 33907
239-939-0639
TheGrammarGranny@aol.com

Dave King
Editor & Contributing Editor
to Writer's Digest Magazine
209 March Road (Ashfield)
Shelburne Falls, MA 01370
413-522-7582
dave@davekingedits.com

Jamie Morris
Writing Coach & Editor
407-644-5163
Jamie@WoodstreamWriters.com
www.WoodstreamWriters.com

Claudette Parmenter
Freelance Writer & Editor
Former Columnist
352-205-4384
cocowriter@yahoo.com

Mary Lois Sanders
Freelance Writer, Editor & Publisher
mary.lois.sanders@att.net
www.courtjesterpublications.com

Tom Wallace
Editor
tommyflorida@earthlink.net
http://home.earthlink.net/-tommyflorida

Children's Literature Specialist:

Paula Morrow
Editing, Ms. Critiquing, Speaking,
Workshops, Publishing (Boxing Day Books)
http://paulamorrow.com

Books:

Finding an **Agent**:

An Agent Speaks: A Primer for Unpublished Writers by Joan West. Fireside Publishers
Guide to Literary Agents, Chuck Sambuchino, Editor. Writer's Digest Books
Jeff Herman's Guide to Book Publishers, Editors, & Literary Agents. Three Dog Press
How to Get a Literary Agent by Michael Larsen. Sourcebooks, Inc.
How to be Your Own Agent by Richard Curtis. Houghton Mifflin Company
Writer's Market, Robert Lee Brewer, Editor. Writer's Digest Books

Writing a **Book Proposal**:

Book Proposals that Sell by Terry Whalin. Write-Now Publications www.right-writing.com
How to Write a Book Proposal by Michael Larsen. Writer's Digest Books
Write the Perfect Book Proposal by Jeff Herman and Deborah M. Adams. John Wiley & Sons, Inc.

Marketing:

First Book Market by Jason Shinder. Macmillian.
Guerrilla Marketing for Writers. Writer's Digest Books
How to Sell Your Books Checklist by Mark H. Newhouse, Amazon.com
How to Sell Your Books Workbook by Linda terBurg. Amazon.com
Publicize Your Book by Jacqueline Deval. A Perigree Book
Sell Your Book like Wildfire: The Writer's Guide to Marketing & Publicity by Rob Eagar. Writer's Digest Books
Writer's Market, Robert Lee Brewer, Editor. Writer's Digest Books

Self-Publishing:

Complete Guide to Self-Publishing (The): Everything you need to know to write, publish, promote and sell your own book by Tom & Marlyn Ross. Writer's Digest Books

Complete Idiot's Guide to Getting Published (The) by Sheree Bykofsky and Jennifer Basye Sander. Alpha

Dan Poynter's Self-Publishing Manual. Para Publishing

Self-Publishing for Dummies by Jason R. Rich. Wiley Publishing, Inc.

On **Writing:**

Complete Guide to Writing Fiction and Nonfiction and Getting it Published, 2nd ed. By Pat Kubis and Bob Howland Prentice Hall

Creating Fiction by Julie Checkoway. Story Press

Curious Case of the Misplaced Modifier (The): How to Solve the Mysteries of Weak Writing by Bonnie Trenga. Writer's Digest Books

Getting the Words Right: How to Rewrite, Edit & Revise by Theodore A. Rees Cheney. Writer's Digest Books

How to Write & Sell Your First Novel by Oscar Collier with Frances Spatz Leighton. Writer's Digest Books

Practical Writer (The): From Inspiration to Publication Edited by Therese Eiben and Mary Gannon with the staff of Poets & Writers Magazine

Self-Editing for Fiction Writers by Renni Browne & Dave King. Harper Resources

Style Guides:

The Chicago Manual of Style, 16th ed. University of Chicago Press

Creative Writer's Style Guide by Christopher T.Leland. Writer's Digest Books

Dash of Style (A): The Art and Mastery of Punctuation by Noah Lukeman W.W. Norton & Company

Roget's Thesaurus 4th ed. Random House

The Elements of Style, 4th ed. by William Strunk, Jr. and E. B. White. Allyn & Bacon

Joan West

Business Books:

Business and Legal Forms for Authors and Self-publishers, 3rd ed. by Ted Crawford. Allworth Press

Law (in Plain English) for Writers by Leonard D. DuBoff, and Bert P. Krages, II Attorneys at Law. Sphinx Publishing (an imprint of Source Books)

Inc. Yourself: How to Profit by Setting up Your Own Corporation, 10th Ed. by Judith H. McQuowan. Career Press

Miscellaneous:

Beginning Writer's Answer Book edited by Jane Friedman. Writer's Digest Books

How to Blog a Book by Nina Amir. Writer's Digest Books

Book Fairs:

Anita Andrews, Exhibits Representative
Association Book Exhibit (Free)
9423 Old Mt. Vernon Road
Alexandria, VA 22309
TEL: 703-619-5030
FAX: 703-619-5035

Newsletters:

Creative Writer's Notebook
Mary Lois Sanders, Editor & Publisher
mary.lois.sanders@att.net
E-mail for subscription information

Helping Writers Succeed
Available January 1213
E-mail firesidepublishers@comcast.net in January for info.
Free

Firstwriter.com/newsletter
Free

Publishing Poynters
Book and Information-Marketing News and Ideas from
Dan Poynter
DanPoynter@ParaPublishing.com
Free

Right Writing News
W. Terry Whalin
Right_Writing_News@right-writing.com
Free

Writer Gazette
Krista Barrett
editor@writergazette.com to subscribe
www.writergazette.com
Free

Websites:

www.absolutewrite.com
www.actionplan.blogs.com
www.authorsden.com
www.blogspot.com
www.filedby.com
www.firstwriter.com
www.hubpages.com
www.theperspiringwriter.com
www.writing.com
www.visualthesaurus.com

Printing and Photos & Illustrations:

www.istockphoto.com
www.printforless.com
www.printrunner.com
www.vistaprint.com

Website Builders:

www.GoDaddy.com
www.weebly.com

Writer's Associations:

Joan West

www.Horror.org (Horror Writer's Organization)
www.Mysterywritersofamerica.com
www.RWA.org (Romance Writers of America

Bibliography of Selected Resources from Chapters:

Amir, Nina. How to Blog a Book. Cincinnati, Ohio:
Writer's Digest Books 2012

Bennett, Lois. Essays on Living with Alzheimer's Disease: The First
Twelve Months. Sommerville, FL: Kadin Books 2010

Berg, A. Scott. Max Perkins: Editor of Genius. New York: Riverhead
Books 1978

Browne, Renni & Dave King. Self-Editing for Fiction Writers: How to
edit yourself into print. 2nd ed. New York: HarperCollins 2004

Carson, Rachel. The Silent Spring. New York: Houghton- Mifflin 1962

CATS: Short Stories about Cats. Joan West, Editor. Lady Lake, Florida:
Fireside Publishers 2009

Cheney, Theodore A. Rees. Getting the Words Right: How to Rewrite,
Edit & Revise. Cincinnati, OH: Writer's Digest Books 1990

Christmas, Bobbie. Purge Your Prose of Problems: A Book Doctor's Desk
Reference. Atlanta, GA: Zebra Communications 2007

Crawford, Ted. Business and Legal Forms for Authors and Self-
publishers, 3rd. Ed. New York: Allworth Press 2004

Didion, Joan. Run, River, New York: Random House 2004

DuBoff, Leonard D. and Bert P. Krages, II Attorneys at Law. Law (in
Plain English) for Writers. Naperville, Illinois: Sphinx Publishing (an
imprint of Source Books) 2005

Joan West

Eagar, Rob. Sell Your Book like Wildfire: The Writer's Guide to
    Marketing & Publicity. Cincinnati, Ohio: Writer's Digest Books
    2012

Fussell, James A. Hallmark puts another nail in the coffin of a dying
    pronoun. McClatchy Newspapers appearing in The Villages Daily
    Sun September 2012

Guide to Literary Agents. Chuck Sambuchino, Editor. Cincinnati, Ohio:
    Writer's Digest Books 2008

Hemingway, Ernest. A Moveable Feast. New York: Scribner   1964

Hermann, Jeff. Jeff Herman's Guide to Book Publishers,   Editors, and
    Literary Agents, Stockton, MA: Three Dog Press 2007

High, Olivia Claire. The Crystal Angel. Lady Lake, Florida: Fireside
    Publishers 2009
    Rose Cottage. Lady Lake, Florida: Fireside Publishers 2010
    Dreams: Shadows of the Night. Summerfield, Florida: Fireside
    Publications 2012

Howard, John H. Faces in the Mirror: Oscar Micheaux & Spike Lee. Lady
    Lake, Florida: Fireside Publications 2009

Kubis, Pat and Bob Howland. The Complete Guide to Writing Fiction and
    Nonfiction and Getting it Published, 2nd ed. Upper Saddle River, NJ:
    Prentice Hall 1990

Lukeman, Noah. A Dash of Style: The Art and Mastery of Punctuation.
    New York: W.W. Norton & Compa, Inc. 2006

McCourt, Frank. Angela's Ashes. New York: Scribner 1996

McQuowan, Judith H. Inc. Yourself: How to Profit by Setting up Your Own Corporation, 10th Ed. Franklin Lakes, New Jersey: Career Press 2004

Masek, Linda Lehmann. The Poison Tree. New York: Avalon Books 2004
Soul Dance. Lady Lake, Florida: Fireside Publishers 2012
The Serpent Sea. Summerfield, Florida: Fireside Publications 2012

Morrison, Toni. Beloved, New York: Alfred A. Knopf 1987

Newhouse, Mark H, How to Sell Your Books Checklist, AimHi Press, 2014

Rendell, Ruth. The Water's Lovely. New York: Crown   Publishers 2006

Roget's Thesaurus 4th ed. New York: Random House 2001

Ross, Tom and Marilyn. The Complete Guide to Self-Publishing: Everything you need to know to write, publish, promote and sell your own book. Cincinnati, Ohio: Writer's Digest Books.

Sayers, Dorothy L. Whose Body? New York: HarperCollins   1923

Stevens, Mary J. Blessed: My Battle with Brain Disease. Lady Lake, Florida: Fireside Publications 2008

terBurg, Linda, How to Sell Your Books Workbook, AimHi Press, 2014

The Chicago Manual of Style, 16th ed. Chicago, IL: University of Chicago Press 2010

Treeson, Ruth. The Long Walk, Lady Lake, Florida: Fireside Publications 2010

Joan West

Trenga, Bonnie. The Curious Case of the Misplaced   Modifier: How to
    Solve the Mysteries of Weak Writing. Cincinnati, OH: Writer's digest
    Books   2006

Updike, John. Couples, N Y: Random House 1968
    Rabbit is Rich, NY: Random House 1981
    Rabbit at Rest, NY: Alfred A. Knopf 1990

West, Joan. An Agent Speaks: A Primer for Unpublished Writers. Lady
    Lake, Florida: Fireside Publications 2010

William Strunk, Jr. and E. B. White, The Elements of Style, 4th ed.
    Needham Heights, MA: Allyn & Bacon 2000

Writer's Market. Robert Lee Brewer, Editor. Cincinnati, Ohio: Writer's
    Digest Books 2011

Zbykofsky, Sherree and Jennifer Basye Sander. The Complete Idiot's
    Guide to Getting Published. New York: the Penguin Group 2006

CONTRACT EXAMPLE:

FIRESIDE PUBLICATIONS INC.
1004 San Felipe Lane
Lady Lake, Florida 32159

Publishing Agreement

This agreement dated is made between Fireside Publications (a small press publisher), hereinafter called Publisher, and,__ hereinafter called Author, as respects, ___, hereinafter called the Work.

I   **Grant of Rights:**

     A.   The Author, on behalf of him/herself and his/her heirs, executors, administrators, successors and assignees, grants to the Publisher: the exclusive worldwide rights to produce, publish, and sell in paperback format as well as electronic, including electronic download, disk, audio tape/CD, E-book reader (including, but not limited to HTML, Palm, Adobe or any other digital format known or that may be invented) the Work in English as well as any foreign rights as may be obtained. Film and/or Television Rights, Radio Rights, Book Club Rights, Direct Mail Rights, First Periodical Rights, Foreign Rights, to be retained by the Author, with the split of royalties upon sale to be 60% to Author and 40% to Publisher.

     B.   To ensure efforts are not duplicated by the Author and/or the Publisher, each party shall notify the other promptly regarding any indication of interest by a third party in obtaining any of the Secondary Rights.

     C.   The Author hereby retains all rights to the Work not specifically granted to the Publisher in this contract.

II   **Author Warrantees:**

     A.   Author warrants that he/she is the author and sole owner of the Work, or has been assigned exclusive rights to the Work; that it is original and contains no matter unlawful in its content; that no part was taken from or based on any other literary, dramatic, or musical material or from any film or graphic arts, except as identified in writing by the Author.

     B.   That the Work does not infringe upon: any copyright, any privacy rights, any other right of a third party, or any common law or statutory law; is not in the public domain, that these rights are owned or controlled by him/her without encumbrance and that the Author has full power to grant the listed rights to the Publisher.

     C.   That the Work does not contain any material of a libelous or obscene nature.

     D.   If this Work has been previously published in any form, Author warrants that exclusive rights granted herein have reverted to him/her. As an addendum to this agreement, Author shall present some written memorandum documenting the reversion of the rights granted by any publishing company that may still own proprietary rights to the Work.

E.   If a judgment is obtained against the Publisher for usurping rights still controlled by another publisher or other entity than the Publisher or the Author, the Author agrees to hold the Publisher harmless and to indemnify the Publisher for reasonable damages and costs. If the Publisher prevails against a suing party or resolves the matter by out of court settlement, the Author will not be liable to indemnify the Publisher for defense and settlement costs

F.   The Author agrees to hold the Publisher harmless and reimburse actual damages awarded to the other party, including costs and attorney's fees, to the publisher against any claim, demand, action, suit, proceeding, or any expense whatsoever arising from claims of infringement of copyright or proprietary right, or claims of libel, obscenity, invasion of privacy, or any other unlawfulness based upon or arising from claims or infringement of copyright or proprietary right, or based upon or arising out of the publication, or any matter to which the Author is a knowing party, pertaining to the Work.

G.   The Author also warrants and represents that, to the best of the Author's knowledge, all statements of fact contained in the Work are true and based on appropriate and diligent research.

H.   The Author also warrants that he/she will not hereinafter enter into any agreement or understanding with any person or entity that would conflict with the rights granted to the Publisher during the term of this contract.

I.   The Author also warrants that in signing this document, he/she is over the age of eighteen and legally able to enter into this transaction per the laws of the State of Florida.

III   **Manuscript:**

A.   The Author agrees to deliver the completed manuscript to the Publisher by___ , along with any rights documentation required for legal contract. Failure to submit proper documentation may result in the withdrawal of the contract offer. Any delays in editing or producing the final manuscript require a discussion with the Publisher. If the Publisher regards the delay to be excessive, this agreement may be terminated.

B.   The specific format of the manuscript will be provided to the Author in a separate document.

C.   The manuscript shall be delivered to the Publisher by means of a read/write CD, transmitted as an email attachment and a paper document. The Author must keep on file a copy of said manuscript in the case of computer failure at the Publisher.

D.   At the time of delivery of the final manuscript, the Author shall include written authorizations or permissions for the use of copyrighted or other proprietary material that appears in the Work, including but not limited to art, illustrations or quotes. These permissions and authorizations shall be obtained at the Author's expense.

E.   The Publisher reserves the right of final approval on final Work submissions. The Author shall be notified of such acceptance within thirty (30) days of receipt of Work or revised Work.

F.   The Publisher reserves the right to edit and revise the Work for any and all uses described under this Agreement, provided the Author's original concept of the Work is not materially altered without the Author's agreement that such changes are necessary for the overall improvement of the Work. If the Author and the Publisher cannot agree about the changes, this Agreement may become void upon the discretion of the Publisher.

G.   The Publisher reserves the right to reject the Work and terminate this Agreement if the Author fails to meet mentioned deadlines, or if the Work does not meet the Publisher's minimum standards of quality.

H.   The Publisher will provide a proofing copy of the Work, for which Author must provide corrections within two weeks or less if agreed upon by the Publisher and the Author. Publisher has the option to delay release or terminate the Agreement as warranted. Publisher may make corrections of typographical errors without the Author's consent.

I.   The Publisher shall, at its own expense, prepare the Work for commerce, by creating the interior and cover design of the Work. The Publisher agrees to consult with the Author to insure that the spirit and integrity of the Work is consistent with the Author's intent.

J.   In the event the Author requests any changes be made to the book's design, interior or cover art, or desires to make substantial changes in the Work after it has been submitted to the printer, the Author agrees to reimburse the Publisher for the additional set-up fees required to republish the Work. The Publisher may refuse any such requests, which delay the release of the Work.

IV   Cover Art and Back Blurb:

A.   Publisher will furnish cover art. Author will provide suggestions for the back blurb and for the cover. Author will furnish an acceptable photograph for use on the back cover. Publisher will give credit to photographer. Publisher is sole owner of all cover artwork provided by the Publisher for the Author's published book.

V   Title:

A.   Publisher has final approval of release title of the Work. Publisher will make every attempt to use the title suggested by the Author, but Publisher has the option to change the release title if Author's suggested title is too similar to any books already in release by Publisher or recent releases from any other publisher or if Publisher deems that a more appropriate title is necessary. In the event of a title change, Author will be given an opportunity to suggest alternative titles.

VI   Formatting:

A.   Publisher will prepare the Work for release. This would include all conversions from the manuscript into print format and other formats, if necessary.

VII   Promotions:

A.   Publisher shall have the right to produce, advertise, promote and publish the Work in a style in which the Publisher deems appropriate to the work, including format, pricing and distributions.

B.   The Author agrees to promote the Work in whatever style is deemed appropriate.

VIII   Copyright:

A.   Author will be responsible for registering the copyright with the U.S. Copyright Office, including payment of any fees and the costs of preparing printed and/or electronic documentation of the Work as required by the U.S. Copyright office. Author will provide a photocopy or facsimile copy of the Copyright certificate to Publisher within 30 days of receipt. Publisher shall be listed as the publisher of the work in all formats agreed upon.

B.   Author understands that if he/she chooses not to register the copyright with the U.S. Copyright office, he/she may be limited in the damages that could be awarded in court if there is a copyright violation. Publisher will place a copyright notice on all versions of the Work, using the year of first release if no other information is available.

IX   Earnings and Statements:

A.   Publisher will set the retail price of the Work, based on length and comparable works. The Publisher agrees to:

1.   Pay the Author a royalty of seven and one-half percent (7 ½%) of the retail price of the book for any copies sold by the Publisher;

2.   Pay the Author a proportional royalty if the book is subsequently reduced in price from the original cover price, provided the reduced sale price exceeds the cost of production;

3.   Allow the Author to purchase up to 100 books at a twenty percent (20%) discount (no royalty will be paid on discounted books). If the author desires to purchase 100 – 300 books at one time, the discount will be 25%, 300 – 499 books 30% or 500 or more books at one time, the discount will be 35%.

4.   Provide the Author with ten (10) free books upon publication.

B.   Royalties shall be calculated and paid no later than forty-five (45) days following the end of the first six-month period following the release of the title. Thereafter, royalties will be paid within forty-five (45) days following the end of each calendar quarter (March, June, September and December). During any quarter in which royalties owed to Author are less than ten ($10) dollars, a sales report will be issued but the monies due will be held and combined with monies for the following quarter.

C.   Royalties will be paid by check drawn on Fireside Publications banking account.

D.   Publisher will provide a written report of sales with each payment.

E.   No royalties will be paid on copies given to Author at no charge or distributed without payment for such reasons as: review, advertising, publicity, promotions, samples or other similar purposes.

F.   Publisher will provide an annual 1099 Misc. Income Tax Form reflecting all royalties paid for the calendar year, providing such royalties total $600 or more. No form will be generated for any amount below $600.

G.   Author is responsible for obtaining State of   sales tax forms and for filing quarterly taxes on all books sold by the Author. The Publisher urges the Author to make such arrangements in advance.

H.   If the Author should pass away during the term of this contract, Publisher will pay subsequent royalties to Author's heirs, assigns or beneficiaries upon receipt of legal documentation, i.e. a Death Certificate and copy of a legal will showing said beneficiary. Should these documents not be produced, the books will remain for sale and the royalties held by the Publisher until documentation is made available.

I.   If your agent passes away during the term of this contract, her partner will take over the contract as Publisher and will continue its terms with the Author. If both partners pass away, any remaining books will be returned to the Author with the Author paying the shipping charges: also, any rights owned by the Publisher will return to the Author.

J.   The Publisher will maintain sales records of products requiring running royalty payments and sold during the term of this contract. The Publisher shall not be required to keep such records beyond three (3) years after each due date for such payments.

X   Term of Contract:

A.   Contract shall be in force from the date it is signed by all parties until seven years (7) from the actual release date of the Work. The contract may be renewed by mutual consent.

B.   If Publisher does not publish and make the Work available for sale within twelve months of the signing of the contract, this contract may become void and all rights revert to the Author.

C.   Publisher may at its discretion, remove the Work from publication or distribution for reasons of poor sales, excessive returns or other reason deemed by the Publisher to be injurious to the Publisher's or the Author's best interests. Publisher shall give notice to the Author of removal from distribution and the reasons for the withdrawal. If the publisher removes the Work from sale, this contract shall terminate and all rights granted shall revert to the Author.

D.   Author may terminate this agreement before the seven-year period by means of a contract buyout. The Author will notify the Publisher ninety (90) days before buyout date with a certified mail notice or other receipted or traceable delivery service, of the intent to exercise the contract buyout option. All rights granted the Publisher would revert to the Author at the time of the buyout, if proper notification has been done. Upon this contract termination through the buyout option, Publisher will remove listing of the Work from its website and all download-based distributors and advise Books in Print that the particular ISBN is no longer in print. The exception to this termination of contract is that Publisher may continue to sell existing stock of print books, but may not create new physical copies upon depletion of its existing stock. The Author will pay to the Publisher the sum of twenty (20) percent of his/her new contract with another traditional publisher or five hundred ($500) dollars, whichever is higher to exercise this buyout option. The Author will be responsible for full payment of damages and customary legal fees as a result of legal action stemming from failure to pay this buyout clause. A payment agreement will be signed and received, in addition to official notice from the publisher or agent, by Fireside Publications prior to release of rights. All rights to the edited Work will revert to the Author without prejudice upon termination of this contract.

E.   Upon termination of the contract, the Publisher retains the right to sell any outstanding print inventory from which the Author will receive the standard applicable royalty on these copies. All e-book/audio versions will be removed in a reasonable time frame, allowing for the practices of third-party distributors.

XI   Author's Name or Pseudonym:

A.   The Author has the exclusive right to the use of his/her name or pseudonym listed as the author in connection with this Work. Publisher will have a non-exclusive right to use the Author's name, likeness and biographical material for the purposes of advertising, publishing and promoting the Work itself.

XII   Ownership of Characters:

A.   Except as allowed under the sections of this agreement governing promotion of the work, the Author owns the characters and controls their use in sequels or series books, whether published by Publisher or another publisher. Publisher will have a non-exclusive right to use the title, and all material, including characters in the Work, for the purpose of advertising, publishing and promotion of the Work.

B.   If the Author writes another Work that is a sequel to the Work covered in this agreement, using an identical theme and/or major characters from the contracted Work, Publisher retains a right of first refusal for the subsequent work. If Publisher does not accept for publication this additional Work within ninety (90) days of submission, it will be considered refused and the Author will be free to market rights to the new work without encumbrance.

XIII   Publishers Name and Trade Mark:

A.   The Author will not have rights to, or in, any trademark, service mark, trade name or logos used by the Publisher, unless expressly permitted to do so in writing. The Author may, with the Publisher's permission, have limited use of Publisher's marks, symbols or name for use in approved promotional material. The Author may use the cover art in his/her promotional material.

B.   The Publisher will allow the Author the right to use one (1) chapter or approved excerpt of the final version of the Work as a promotional tool on the Author's website. The Author's website must include a link to the website of the Publisher.

XIV   Entire Agreement:

A.   This contract hereby constitutes the entire agreement between the Author and the Publisher, and supersedes all previous agreement regarding the Work, whether oral or in writing. Modification of this agreement may only occur in writing, signed by both parties.

Author's Name:

Writing As:

Address:

Phone:

Cell:

Email:

Website:

Social Security Number:

Working Title of Work:

Signature of Author: _____   Date:_____

Signature of Fireside Publications Agent _____Date:_____

Typed Name of Fireside Representative:

A PUBLISHER SPEAKS:

Helping Writers Succeed

By

Joan West

Joan West   51,368 words
100 Writers Lane
The City, Florida
35997
www.firesidepublishers.com
firesidepublishers@comcast.net
400-400-4000 - Office
300-300-3000 - Cell

(Example of a cover sheet for a nonfiction proposal.)

SAMPLE OF A MARKETING PLAN:
Marketing *Love Tag* by Peter Schianna
12/11 to present

1. Multiple email announcements
2. Author Marketing Experts publicity campaign (three highly favorable reviews)
3. Face-to-face personal contacts
4. Book signing in hometown (Illinois)
5. Local book signing
6. Submission to Royal Palm Literary Award competition (Won First Place!)
7. Interview for local paper
8. RPLA celebration open house
9. Press releases to regional magazines and newspapers
10. Internet video trailer
11. Professionally designed website (www.petershianna.com)
12. Upload as online print and e-book

Going forward

1. Will focus on libraries and writers' groups in Central Florida for readings and talks

Will do 18 readings/talks by June 1 with heavy promotion of RPLA prize

Scheduled—
1. January 28 Belleview Library
2. March   1 Lady Lake Library (table at grand opening of new library
3. TBA   Bushnell Public Library
4. TBA   Citrus Ridge Public Library
5. TBA   Cooper Memorial Library
6. TBA   Sunshine Scribblers (writers' group)
7. TBA   Tippecanoe Arts Federation (Indiana)

2. February 19 Booth at Authors & Book Lovers Showcase

3. Resend press releases with RPLA information

4. Follow up press releases with phone calls

5. Signings and readings in book stores

Joan West

Fireside Publications
1004 San Felipe Lane, Lady Lake, Florida 32159
www.firesidepubs.comcast; firesidepubs@comcast.net
300-300-3000

FOR IMMEDIATE RELEASE

A Sparkling Romantic Suspense Debut Novel by California Writer

The Crystal Angel

Lady Lake, FL/July 9, 2009 – Fireside Publications (www.firesidepubs.com) is proud to announce the publication of debut romantic suspense novel, *The Crystal Angel* by Northern California writer Olivia Claire High. With 248 pages of love, murder, intrigue and the glitter of wealth packed within its covers, High recounts the explosive relationship between interior designer Kemble Morgan and arrogant multi-millionaire Archer Griffith.

Flying between Miami and the exotic island of Barbados, Kemble and Archer carry on their passionate love affair with barbs one minute and kisses the next, all the while defending themselves against mysterious assailants. Who do they have to fear? Is it Nate, the islander with a grudge or beautiful Leslie Craymore, whose family represents old money in Barbados and who has more than a passing interest in Archer?

And, what part does the lovely crystal angel Archer gave to Kemble have to play? Drawn to its beauty, but bewildered by her intense inner link to the figurine, Kemble senses the statue will become more than a beautiful addition to her angel collection. For Kemble, who has the unusual talent for discovering hidden secrets in houses and people, the feeling is intensely unsettling. Whether in Kemble's studio in Miami or Archer's summer home on the shores of the Caribbean, the reader is led through the passion and intrigue of their story.

The book is available on Amazon.com or the publisher's website www.firesidepubs.com. A review copy can be provided. Contact Joan West, Sr. Ed., firesidepubs@comcast.net.
The author is available for telephone interviews.

About the Author

Olivia Claire High was born in Waukegan, Illinois, grew up in San Francisco, California and lived on Guam for a year. Currently residing in northern California with her husband, Joe, the couple have three grown daughters and four grandchildren. A public school teacher for nineteen years, Olivia holds a B.A. degree in Liberal Studies and a Multiple Subjects teaching credential. She enjoys traveling, reading and writing. A member of Romance Writers of America, she is now concentrating on her passion for writing romance and is currently working on her next novel.

Book Statistics

Title:	The Crystal Angel
Author:	Olivia Claire High
ISBN:	978-0-9814672-7-6
Category:	Romantic Suspense
Length:	248 pages
Retail Price:	$13.95
Size:	5.5 x 8.5 paperback
Binding:	Perfect

(NOTE: I've reduced the type sizes on the above to bring it from its original 8 ½ X 11 format to this smaller format. In the original everything above the Book Statistics fit on one page with the Book Statistics and cover image only falling on the second page.)

Joan West

PROPOSAL CHECKLIST

Proposal for: _____

_____	Cover Sheet
_____	Proposal's Table of Contents
_____	Introduction/The Overview
_____	Markets for the Book
_____	Subsidiary rights
_____	Spin Offs
_____	Promotion
_____	Mission Statement
_____	The Author's Platform
_____	Promotion Plan
_____	Competing Books
_____	Resources Need to Complete the Book
_____	About the Author
_____	The Outline/List of Chapters
_____	Sample Chapters
_____	Appendix
_____	Photographs
_____	Other

NOTES AND COMMENTS:

BENNETT & WEST LITERARY AGENCY
1004 San Felipe Lane
Lady Lake, Florida 32159

SUBMISSION GUIDELINES

Manuscript: Type -Double-spaced; **Exception:** Synopsis should be single-spaced.
Double -double-space between scenes <u>ONLY.</u>
Use paper at least 20# weight
Start chapters 1/3 to ½ way down the page.
Header last name title in upper left hand corner each page
Page number in upper right hand corner of every page.
Type the word count in upper left corner of first page.
FONT: Use **12 point Times New Roman** or **Courier** or **Dark**
A cover sheet with your **full name, address, phone number, email address, title, & word count**
DO NOT PUT A COPYRIGHT NOTATION ANYWHERE <u>Don't try to be cute</u>
<u>Don't "package" your material:</u> No binders, no fancy covers.
Send your MS loose -A rubber band is permissible
<u>Don't send attachments</u> - without permission
Telephone only when absolutely necessary.

More about manuscripts:
Proofread it before you send it
Hire an editor if possible
Or invest in a book such as
**<u>Self-Editing for Fiction Writers: How to Edit
yourself into print (2nd ed.)</u>** by Renni Browne & Dave King,
HarperCollins, NY (2004)
There are other excellent books (and some not so excellent) on writing and, no matter how good you think you are, studying a good book can't hurt.

Remember: An agent's job is to sell your book. But she can't send it to editors with a lot of mistakes in it. The more time an agent has to spend helping you edit your work, the longer it takes to get the book to the marketplace.

About the Author

From a stay-at-home mom to an analyst for a fortune five hundred corporation and back to college for a doctorate to put on the hat of a college professor, Joan West has moved from one career to another.

After retiring from teaching, she expanded on the article writing niche she had carved out for herself into writing a novel. As a member of a writers' group, she felt that new authors were receiving short shrift from agents and editors and decided to try her hand as a literary agent. After much research, she joined hands with Lois Bennett to form Bennett and West Literary Agency. The two placed many of their clients' manuscripts into the hands of publishers, but with the advent of perceived chaos in the publishing industry, it became more and more clear that new, untried authors were not particularly welcome.

With a feeling of "if you can't beat 'em, join 'em," Joan and Lois embarked on the adventure of operating a small press publishing company, Fireside Publications. Her first nonfiction book, *An Agent Speaks: A Primer for Unpublished Writers,* is followed by this one, *A Publisher Speaks*: *Helping Writers Succeed*, which continues her mission of—what else—helping writers succeed.

Joan lives in Florida with her editor husband, Glen.

Contact Joan at: firesidepublishers@comcast.net. Put Joan West in the subject line.

Order More Copies of <u>How to Sell Your Books: A Publisher Speaks</u> from createspace.com or amazon.com.

ALSO FROM AIMHIPRESS: available now at createspace.com and amazon.com

HOW TO SELL YOUR BOOKS CHECKLIST
By Mark H. Newhouse

This collection of marketing checklists, useful information, appendices and forms is designed to help any author market and sell their own books. The books in this series are designed for you to tame the marketing monster and find your audience! This is a simple to use logical checklist for marketing that serves as a great companion to <u>How to SELL Your Books MARKETING WORKBOOK</u> and <u>A Publisher Speaks</u>.

HOW TO SELL YOUR BOOKS WORKBOOK
by Linda terBurg

A concise nine month strategy for promoting your books that serves as a great companion to <u>How to SELL Your Books MARKETING CHECKLIST</u> and <u>A Publisher Speaks</u>.

Joan West

Disclaimer

This book is not a be-all or an end-all for the writer hoping to have his book published. I write it to complement, amplify and supplement other texts and I urge you to read all available material in order for you to learn as much as you can about all methods of publishing, including traditional and the various means of non-traditional publishing such as self-publishing and electronic books. The appendix to this book contains as many resources as I could put together. They are scattered throughout the book as well. I wrote the book to provide information regarding the field of publishing, but I don't offer legal opinions in any way. For that you must consult an attorney. I've attempted to make the information in the book as complete and accurate as possible. I will proof read it and edit is, as I advise you to do with all of your writings, but mistakes do happen and you may find a typo or two, if you do, I'd appreciate it if you would let me know. Similarly, I've tried to be as careful as possible in the correctness of the content and believe that I have; however, things change quickly in the publishing business. There will be places where you will want to check before you take action, where a given editor now is or what the online sites rules are currently, etc.

The purpose of this book is to inform and entertain. The author and publisher shall have neither liability nor responsibility to any person or entity with respect to any loss or damage caused, or alleged to have been caused, directly or indirectly, by the information contained in this book. If you do not wish to be bound by the above, you may return this book to the publisher for a full refund.

www.ingramcontent.com/pod-product-compliance
Lightning Source LLC
Chambersburg PA
CBHW070640290526
45790CB00001B/145